BACKGAMMON
FOR
WINNERS

BACKGAMMON FOR WINNERS

Bill Robertie

CARDOZA PUBLISHING

Cardoza Publishing is the foremost gaming publisher in the world with a library of almost 100 up-to-date and easy-to-read books and strategies. These authoritative works are written by the top experts in their fields and with more than 6,500,000 books in print, represent the best-selling and most popular gaming books anywhere.

THIRD EDITION

Visit our new web site (www.cardozapub.com) or write us for a full list of Cardoza books, advanced and computer strategies.

CARDOZA PUBLISHING

PO Box 1500 Cooper Station, New York, NY 10276
Phone (800)577-WINS • Fax (718)743-8284
email: cardozapub@aol.com
www.cardozapub.com

ABOUT THE AUTHOR

Bill Robertie is the world's best backgammon player and the only two-time winner of the Monte Carlo World Championships. Robertie is the author of seven backgammon books and the co-publisher of *Inside Backgammon*, the leading backgammon magazine.

Robertie is also a chess master, a winner of the U.S. Speed Chess Championship, and the author of six chess books.

Robertie's club and tournament winnings from backgammon have allowed him to travel the world in style. He currently makes his home in Arlington, Massachusetts.

BACKGAMMON AND CHESS BOOKS
BY BILL ROBERTIE
501 Essential Backgammon Problems
Backgammon for Winners
Backgammon for Serious Players
Advanced Backgammon Volume 1: Positional Play
Advanced Backgammon Volume 2: Technical Play
Lee Genud vs. Joe Dwek
Reno 1986
Beginning Chess Play
Winning Chess Tactics
Winning Chess Openings
Master Checkmate Strategy
Basic Endgame Strategy: Kings, Pawns, & Minor Pieces
Basic Endgame Strategy: Queens and Rooks

TABLE OF CONTENTS

INTRODUCTION

Welcome to backgammon–the world's oldest, cruelest, most popular, and most exciting game. Does that sound like a lot of superlatives? It sure does–and they're all true.

Cruelest? How cruel can a game be? Until you play backgammon for awhile, you'll have no idea. No game is finished until the two armies break contact and race for the finish line. Players who've been playing for a few years will tell you incredible stories of dead-won positions that were ruined by the most amazing series of long-shot rolls. In fact, at some tournaments there are formal competitions for the best hard-luck stories. Every player has his own storybook of miraculous wins and nightmarish losses. After awhile, you'll have a few of your own– I guarantee it.

Backgammon's easy to learn and in my first two chapters, I'll show you all you need to know to set up a board and play a game with a friend– in just 15 or 20 minutes you'll be up and running.

In this book, I'm going to introduce you to my style. It's based on what I call **dynamic** play–taking some chances early to reap big rewards later. Opening play is the foundation of later success, so in Chapter 4, we'll look at dynamic openings. Chapters 5 and 6 are the meat of the book–two complete games, with diagrams and comments after nearly every move. A good game of backgammon is like a well-conducted military maneuver. In these two chapters, we'll oversee the plan of attack, and see how a well-constructed opening plan can pave the way to a decisive victory.

If you're like most people, this book will just whet your appetite for more. In the final chapters, we'll introduce you to the club and tournament scene, and give you some pointers for future improvement.

The luckiest thing I ever did in my life was learn how to play backgammon. That's a move you're about to make, and I hope it's just as lucky for you, too.

THE BASICS OF PLAY

INTRODUCTION

Most board games fall into one of two general types: the **war games,** or games of maneuver, encirclement and capture (chess and checkers are the most popular examples), and **race games** such as backgammon, where the objective is to outrace your opponent around some sort of track or layout.

Backgammon is by far the most popular of the race games. Each player has an army of 15 pieces, also called **checkers** or **men**, which move around a board consisting of 24 triangular **points**. The points are similar to squares on a chessboard, except that each point can hold any number of men from the same army.

THE PLAYERS

Backgammon is played by two opposing players, but unlike chess or checkers, it makes no difference what color pieces you play–either color is equally likely to make the first move.

THE EQUIPMENT

To play backgammon, you need the following equipment:

• A backgammon board.

• Thirty round checkers, fifteen each of two different colors. The checkers are often referred to as **men** or **pieces**.

• Two pairs of dice. Usually, dice with rounded corners are used, although this is not strictly necessary.

• Two dice cups, for shaking and throwing the dice. The best dice cups have a small lip, or raised surface just inside the mouth of the cup, to guarantee that the dice are rolling when they leave the cup.

• **A doubling cube**, a six-sided cube with the numbers 2, 4, 8, 16, 32 and 64 on the six faces. This keeps track of the number of units at stake in the game.

THE BACKGAMMON BOARD

Backgammon boards vary widely in price and quality. You can buy an inexpensive board at your local game department store for just a few dollars. You can spend about $100 and get a full tournament-sized set with a playing surface of cork or cloth. Or, if you're feeling wealthy or just extravagant, you can spend over $1000 for beautiful leather boards with contrasting leather and brass accessories.

Most backgammon sets fold in half for convenience. Clubs, however, sometimes purchase solid sets made from one piece of wood. And some sets are even inlaid into table tops. Whatever your choice, you should invest in a backgammon set and use it to play along with the examples in this book. You'll find that learning the concepts is much easier if you actually take the time to move real pieces about on a real board.

Diagram 1 shows a backgammon board, with each point numbered 1- 24.

Diagram 1: A Backgammon Board

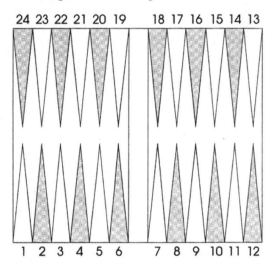

The board is divided into four sections, or **quadrants**, with six points in each quadrant. Running down through the middle of the board is a raised section known as the **bar**. The bar is not a point but instead, is a resting place for checkers that have been **hit**, or captured, during the course of play. Once a checker has been hit, it is placed on the bar, and must first reenter in the farthest quadrant before any other pieces can move.

HOW TO SET UP THE BOARD

Diagram 2 shows the initial placement of the pieces at the beginning of the game. Black has two pieces on the point labelled **24**, three pieces on point **8**, and five pieces on points **6** and **13**. White's position is the mirror image of Black's. He has two checkers on point **1**, three on point **17**, and five each on points **12** and **19**.

Diagram 2: Starting Position

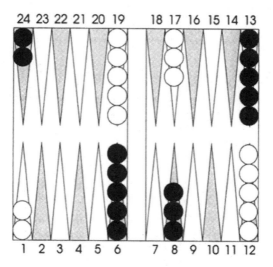

THE DIRECTION OF MOVEMENT

The two armies race around the board in opposite directions. Diagram 3 shows the direction of movement of the two armies.

Diagram 3: Direction of Movement

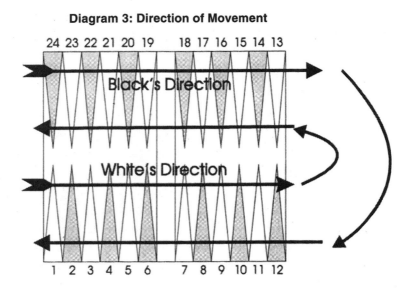

Black checkers move in a clockwise direction, from the upper left to the upper right quadrants, then down to the lower right quadrant and finally to the lower left quadrant. The White checkers move in the opposite direction.

Notice that the top and bottom halves of the board are connected along the right-hand side: a Black piece moving to the point numbered 13 in the diagram moves next to the point numbered 12, and then along to 11 and so forth. A White piece moving along the bottom of the board to point 12 will next move to point 13, and then to the left along the top edge of the board.

HOW TO MOVE THE PIECES

In backgammon, the two players take turns moving. To make a move, a player puts two dice in his cup, shakes them, and rolls the dice out onto the right-hand side of the board. He then moves his checkers corresponding to the numbers on the dice.

Suppose, for instance, it is your turn and you roll a 3 and a 1. You can move two separate checkers, or you can make your whole move with one checker. You may move one checker three spaces forward and another checker one space forward, or one checker a total of four spaces forward. This is not quite the same as having a move of four spaces as we shall see, for each die must be played individually.

Look at Diagram 4. Black has a 3-1 to play. (Remember that Black moves clockwise around the board). He elects to move one checker from the 13-point to the 10-point (a total of three spaces) and another checker from the 24-point to the 23-point (one space). The resulting position is shown in Diagram 5.

Diagram 4: Black to play a 3-1

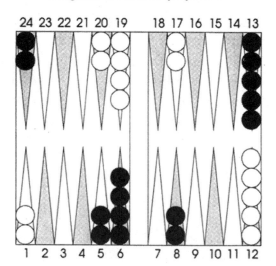

**Diagram 5: Position after Black has played
13 to 10 and 24 to 23**

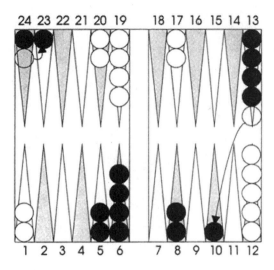

In Diagram 6, White has a 4-2 to play. He elects to move one checker four spaces from the 17-point to the 21-point (White moves in the opposite direction from Black) and one checker two spaces from the 19-point to the 21-point. Diagram 7 shows the position after White has played the 4-2.

Diagram 6: White has a 4-2 to play

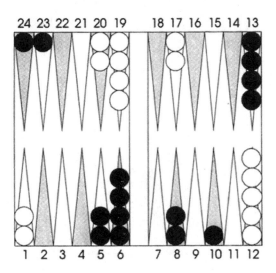

Diagram 7: White has played the 4-2

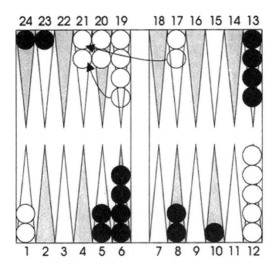

DOUBLES

Up to now we've looked at what happens when you throw two different numbers on the dice. Suppose, however, that the same number comes up on both dice? That's called throwing **doubles**, and it's very good for you.

When you throw doubles, you get to play the number, not just twice, but four times! In most positions, this gives you a powerful jump on your opponent, and in fact, if you throw more doubles than your opponent, you will probably win the game.

Diagram 8: Black to play 44

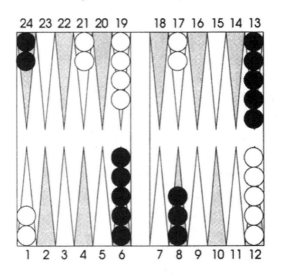

In Diagram 8, Black has thrown double-4s. He has many ways to play the number, all of which are good for him. One of the best is to use two of his 4s to bring both men from the 24-point to the 20-point, and the other two 4s to bring two men from the 13-point to the 9-point. The resulting position is shown in Diagram 9.

Diagram 9: Position after Black plays 44

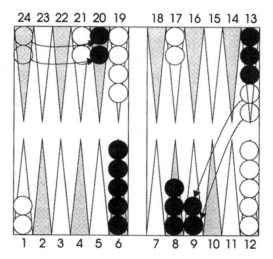

POINTS

Two checkers of the same color on a point constitute a **made point**, or simply a **point**. The opposing player cannot land on that point by an exact count, although he may hop over the point and move beyond it.

Diagram 10: Black to play 53

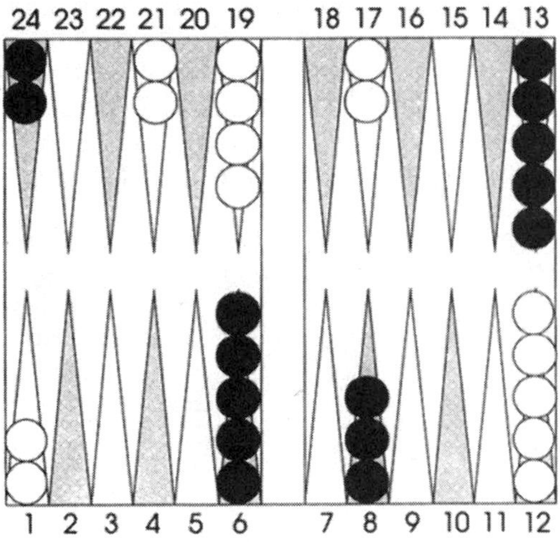

Look at Position 10. Black has a 5-3 to play. Notice that he cannot move either of the checkers on the 24-point. He can't move them 3 spaces, because the point 3 spaces away is the 21-point, and White has made that point with two of his checkers. He also can't move the checkers 5 spaces, because the point 5 spaces away is the 19-point, and White has made that point with four of his checkers. So the checkers on the 24-point can't move either part of the roll, although the point 8 spaces away, the 16-point, is still wide open.

Several points in a row constitute a **prime**. Six points in a row is a **full prime**, and any checkers caught behind a full prime are trapped until the prime is broken.

You must always play both parts of your throw if you can. Take a look at Diagram 11. Black has a 6-4 to play.

Notice that if Black plays his 4 first, from 24 to 20, then he has no 6 to play anywhere on the board! This isn't legal. Black could play either 24 to 18 and 13 to 9, or 13 to 9 to 3. But he must use his whole throw if he can.

Diagram 11: Black has a 6 and 4 to play

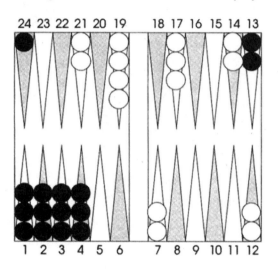

Sometimes a position arises where a player can play one number or the other, but not both.

Look at Diagram 12 on the next page.

Diagram 12: Black to play 65

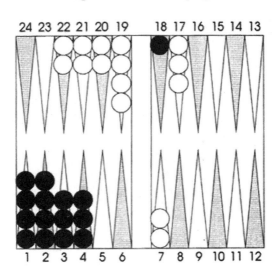

Black has a 6 and a 5 to play. If he decides to play the 6, he will have no legal 5, but if he plays the 5, he will have no 6! In this case, Black **must** play the larger of the two numbers. His only legal play is from 18 to 12, stopping there.

BLOTS

A **blot** is a single checker on a point. While two men on a point constitute a strong fortress that can restrain an opponent, a blot is a vulnerable weakness, which can be hit and sent back to the beginning of the race.

Look at Diagram 13 on the next page.

Diagram 13

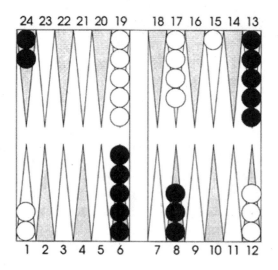

White has a blot on the 15-point. Black now rolls a 6-3. He can take one of his checkers on the 24-point, move it to the 15-point using his entire roll, and *hit* the White blot. The White blot now moves from the 15-point to the *bar* (the raised area in the center of the board).

The resulting position is shown in Diagram 14 on the next page.

Diagram 14. Position after White has been hit

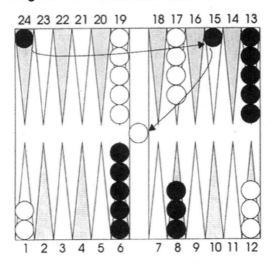

ENTERING FROM THE BAR

The bar is a sort of holding pen, where White and Black checkers that have been hit are placed to restart their race around the board. Once a checker is on the bar, no other checker can be moved until that checker has been reentered onto the board. White's checkers must enter in Black's home board (points 1-6). Black's checkers enter in White's home board (points 24-19).

Let's look at Diagram 14 again. White has been sent to the bar and must now enter before he can make any move with his other pieces. Suppose his next roll is a 2-6. This gives him a 2 and a 6 to play. He could use the 2 to enter his checker from the bar to the 2-point, which is open.

But notice that he can't use the 6 to enter, because the 6-point is a made point and belongs to Black. So half of

White's move is forced–he has to use his 2 to place the checker from the bar to the 2-point. He can now make any legal 6 he wishes. Suppose he plays a checker from the 1-point to the 7-point. The resulting position is shown in Diagram 15.

Diagram 15. Position after White played 62

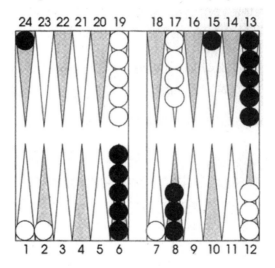

THE OPENING ROLL

To begin the game, each player puts one die in his cup, shakes it, and rolls the die out into his right-hand half of the board. The player who throws the larger number moves first, and his roll is the combination of the two dice. For example: you and I are playing. You roll a five, and I roll a three. You have the opening roll, and you must play a 5-3.

Some players play with the rule of **automatic doubles**: if both players roll the same number on the opening throw, the cube is turned to 2 and the players roll again. However, this is an optional rule.

THE OBJECT OF THE GAME

When playing backgammon, your objective is to take all your checkers off the board before your opponent. Before you can take any checkers off the board, however, you must first maneuver all your checkers into your own **inner board**. In the diagrams that we've been using, the points labelled 1 through 6 are **Black's inner board** or **home**, while the points labelled 19 through 24 are **White's inner board** or **home**.

Once all 15 of your checkers are in your own inner board, you may begin **bearing off**. (See explanation below). If you bear off all your checkers before your opponent, but your opponent gets at least one checker off, you win a **single game**, worth 1 point. If you bear off all your checkers before your opponent bears off any checkers, you win a **gammon**, or **double game**, worth 2 points.

And, if you bear off all your checkers and your opponent still has one or more checkers on the bar or in your inner board, you win a **backgammon**, or **triple game**, worth 3 points!

BEARING OFF

The object of the game is to bear all your checkers off the board before your opponent. However, you cannot bear off any checkers until all your checkers are in your **home board**.

Diagram 16

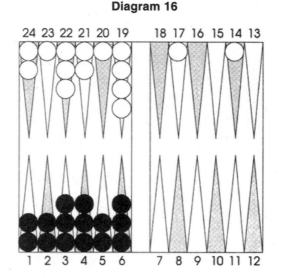

Black's home board are the points labelled 1- 6; White's home board are points 19 through 24. In Diagram 16, Black has already maneuvered all his men home. White, on the other hand, still has two men in his outer board. Black can start bearing off immediately; White still has to move those two outside men home.

To bear off, you roll the dice and remove men corresponding to the numbers thrown. For example, if Black throws a 5 and a 3 in Diagram 16, he may remove a checker from his 5-point and a checker from his 3-point. Once removed, a checker can never be returned to play.

You are not, however, compelled to remove checkers with the numbers thrown. With the 5-3 roll, Black could, if he wished, play a checker from his 6-point to his 1-point and a checker from his 5-point to his 2-point.

However, this would not be as good as removing checkers from the board.

If you roll a number higher than the highest occupied point, you may use it to bear a checker off the highest occupied point. Look at Diagram 17.

Diagram 17. Black to play 64

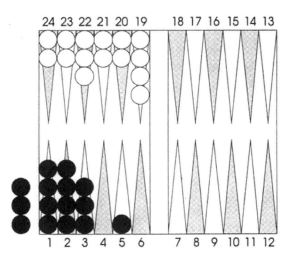

In this case, Black has no checkers on either the 6-point or the 4-point. He can use the 6 to bear off the checker from the 5-point, and then use the 4 to bear off his checker on the 3-point. If, in the process of bearing off, you leave a blot and your opponent hits you, you must first reenter that checker and bring it around to your home board before bearing off any other checkers.

Look at Diagram 18.

Diagram 18

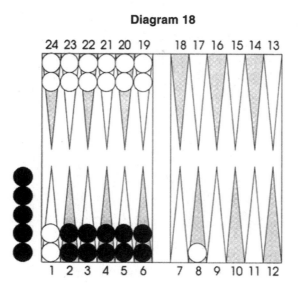

Black has been rolling well and has only 10 checkers left. White, on the other hand, is in bad shape. He's way behind, and might conceivably lose a gammon or a backgammon. Watch how quickly the tables can turn.

In Diagram 18, Black rolls 65. With the 6, he has to play a checker off the 6-point, leaving a vulnerable blot. With the 5, he would like to move that blot to a safe point, but he can't; the point five away from the 6-point is the 1-point, and White owns that. The only other play with the 5 is to take a checker off the 5-point, leaving another vulnerable blot!

Look at Diagram 19 on the next page.

Diagram 19. Black has just played 65

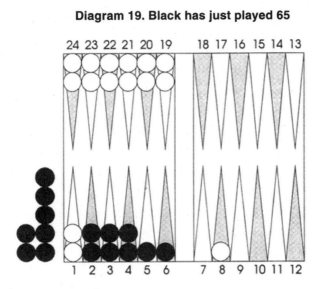

Black's left himself wide open and White pounces, rolling a 54! With the 5, he plays from the 1-point to the 6-point, hitting Black's blot and sending it to the bar. With the 4, he plays from the 1-point to the 5-point, hitting the other blot.

The new position is shown in Diagram 20 on the next page.

Diagram 20. Black has two checkers on the bar

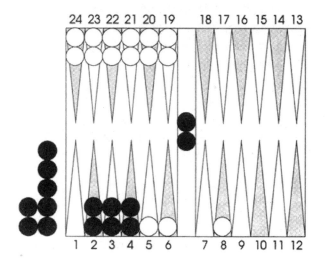

What can Black do? He has to enter checkers from the bar before he can move any others. But he has to enter in White's home board (the points numbered 19 through 24), and White owns all those points! No matter what number Black throws, it will correspond to a point that White has made.

White's position is known as a **closed board**, and as long as White maintains this position, Black has no chance of entering and has to forfeit his turn.

The future course of this game is pretty clear. White will move his three remaining checkers around and in to his home board. Eventually, he will start removing checkers, and as he does, he will open up some of the points which he now controls. Once he does, Black can try to enter.

Even after Black enters both his men, however, he will have to move them around and back into his home board before he can start bearing off again. That's going to take a long time, however, so right now White is a big favorite to win the game. That's backgammon: a single stroke of bad luck (or good luck, depending on your point of view) can turn an apparently overwhelming position into a disaster.

THE DOUBLING CUBE

In the 1920s, some unknown genius, probably living in the New York area, created something which forever changed the way backgammon was played: the **doubling cube**. With the addition of the doubling cube (backgammon players just refer to it as "the cube") backgammon became a quicker, more exciting game–the best two-player game in the world.

The doubling cube works like a raise in poker. If you like your position, you may raise the stakes, hoping to either drive the opposing player out of the game, or force him to accept a disadvantageous position at double the stakes.

The doubling cube is slightly larger than the dice used to determine the moves, and has the numbers 2, 4, 8, 16, 32 and 64 on its six sides. The cube is used to determine the value of the game (in a game played for money) or the number of points won or lost (in a tournament match).

At the beginning of a game, the doubling cube is placed between the two players with the number 64 facing up. Since there is no "1" on the cube, this indicates that the value of the game is currently 1 point. When one player feels that he has a solid advantage, he may choose to double the value of the game. He does this by saying *I double*, or something to that effect, and placing the cube on his opponent's side of the board with the number "2" facing up.

The second player now has a choice. He may feel he is a big underdog, and give up the game. In this case, he says *I drop*, and the game is finished. The player who doubled wins one point (the previous value of the cube).

Perhaps, however, the second player feels he still has a fighting chance to win. In this case he may say *I take*, or *I accept* and place the cube on his side of the board. He now *owns* the cube. The game continues, but the value of a single game is now doubled, 2 points. A gammon is now worth 4 points, and a backgammon is worth 6 points. Once the initial double has been made, only the player who owns the cube has the right to redouble.

Suppose that after some rolls, the second player feels that the position has turned in his favor. In this case he may, before he rolls the dice, redouble the game by turning the cube to 4 and offering it back to the first player. The first player may now give up the game and lose 2 points, or play on by accepting the cube at 4. In this case a single game is now worth 4 points, a gammon is worth 8 points, and a backgammon, 12 points!

Theoretically, this doubling and redoubling could continue for quite a while. In practice, between experienced players, the cube rarely gets beyond the 4 level. However, every veteran player has experienced a few games where the cube has reached 32 (or more)!

DYNAMIC OPENINGS

INTRODUCTION

In this section, we'll show you how to play dynamic backgammon so that right from the opening you're in control. **Dynamic play** lets you set the pace and determine the course the game will take. **Passive play**, on the other hand, lets your opponent call the shots. That's not what we want. In this section, we'll show you how to play your openings so you're in control.

Before we look at how to play particular rolls, however, we need to step back for a minute and consider the big picture. What are our goals in the opening? What are we trying to do?

WINNING GOALS

Let's look again at Diagram 2, the starting position. Take a good look at Black's checkers. His goal, remember, is to maneuver all 15 of his checkers into his home board (points 1-6 in the diagram), then bear them off. And he needs to do all this before White does the same thing. Of his 15 checkers, five are already in his home board–the five located on the 6-point. Three others are close by, on the 8-point. And five others are located not too far away, on the 13-point.

These 13 checkers constitute the bulk of Black's army,

and they don't have far to go to get home. What's more, because they're close to each other, they can cooperate in making new points. With a throw of 3-1, for instance, Black can move one checker from the 6-point and the 8-point to make the 5-point. In the same way, a throw of 4-2 will make the 4-point, and a throw of 6-1 will make the 7-point (also known as the **bar-point**, because it's located right next to the bar in the middle of the board).

That's good news for those 13 checkers. They're close to home, and they support each other by being able to make new points. But what about Black's other two checkers?

Take a look at those other two checkers. They're stuck wr y back on the 24-point–a long way from the rest of Black's army. In order to connect with the rest of Black's forces, those checkers are going to have to make their way through a minefield –the 23 through the 14-points, an area which is pretty well controlled by **White's** army.

That, in a nutshell, is the real problem in the opening of a backgammon game–how to get your rear checkers forward to join the rest of your army, while White is doing his best to control their escape route and either hit them and send them back to the bar, or block their escape route by making new points. White, of course, has the very same problem. His rear checkers are trying to get out of your **home board**, through your **outer board** (the 7 through 12-points), and home to safety. The opening of most backgammon games is a constant seesaw struggle, with both players trying to simultaneously block and hit their opponent's men while mobilizing their own.

Here are the <u>Four Key Opening Goals</u>.

FOUR KEY OPENING GOALS
1. Hit Your Opponent's Men

This is key. When you can hit a checker, it's usually right to do it. Since your opponent's checker has to go to the bar and then reenter your home board *before he can do anything else*, you gain time in the race. If your opponent rolls some unlucky numbers, he might have to stay on the bar and lose a whole turn or two. That could give you time to escape with your backmen.

2. Build Blocking Points

This is very important, although usually a little less important than hitting your opponent. (But not always!) Every blocking point makes it more difficult for your opponent's back men to escape. The longer you can keep those back men trapped, the bigger your advantage.

3. Build An Anchor

What's an **anchor**, you ask? Answer: an advanced point in your opponent's home board. From Black's point of view, the 20-point, the 21-point, or the 18-point would constitute an anchor. If Black can move his two back men up to one of those points, he would have a strong defensive position which would be hard to block. Black could then bide his time and look for a chance to run home later.

4. Mobilize Your Checkers

By **mobilize**, I mean move your checkers into positions where they more easily accomplish goals 1-3. For instance, with a 4 on the dice you might move a back checker from the 24-point to the 20-point (hoping to make an anchor there next turn); with a 3 you might bring a checker from the 13-point to the 10-point (hoping to make a new blocking point the following turn). Since neither player has many dice throws on the opening turn to directly accomplish one of our first three goals, these *mobilization* plays are critical.

That's the overall picture. In the opening, you're trying to block, anchor, hit, and mobilize–**BAHM** for short. Now let's see how you'd play each of your 15 possible opening rolls. Remember, since you have to *win* the opening roll by throwing a bigger number than your opponent, you can't start the game with a double. Also, you can't do any hitting on the opening roll–in the starting position, neither you nor your opponent have any blots. (That situation will quickly change, however.)

THE OPENING MOVES

THE BLOCKING ROLLS:
3-1, 4-2, 5-3, and 6-1

3-1: Make the 5-point

The best opening shot is 3-1. Use it to make your 5-point, as in Diagram 21:

Diagram 21. Black has played a 3-1

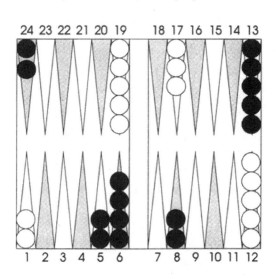

With this roll you accomplish two things: you make a blocking point, further hemming in White's two checkers on your 1-point, and you make an *inner- board point*.

The extra importance of an inner-board point (as opposed to a point in your outer board, like the 10-point) is simply this: if you hit your opponent at some point in the future, which you are likely to do, he will no longer be able to reenter the game when he throws a 5 on the dice, because that point now belongs to you.

Since you own the 6-point as well, your opponent will need to throw one of the numbers 1, 2, 3, or 4, to reenter from the bar. That may sound easy to do, but in fact by making that second point in your board, you quadrupled the number of dice throws that leave your opponent on the bar! When you only owned the 6-point, only one dice throw left White on the bar: 6-6. Now that you own the 5 and 6-points, a total of four throws will leave White on the bar: 6-6, 5-5, 6-5, and 5-6.

In the Middle East, where backgammon originated, inner points are called **doors**, because you have to enter through them to get back in the game. When *all* the doors are shut, you're closed out, and can't get back in the game.

4-2: Make the 4-point

The second-best opening roll is a 4-2, which you should use to make the 4-point, as in Diagram 22 on the next page:

Diagram 22: Black has played 4-2

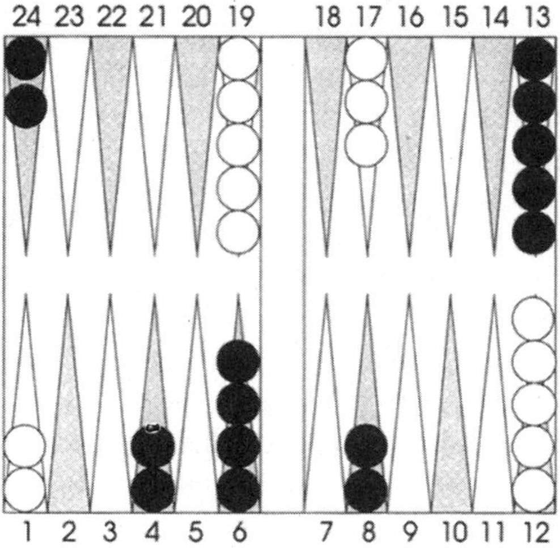

4-2 is a great opening roll for pretty much the same reasons as 3-1. It's not quite as good as 3-1 for this reason: after you make the 4-point, White still has a chance to sneak behind you and bring his back men up to the 5-point. If he can do that, the value of the 4-point will be somewhat negated.

This illustrates another important backgammon principle: *consecutive points are stronger than points with gaps in between.*

5-3: Make the 3-point
5-3 isn't as good an opening roll as 3-1 or 4-2, for an obvious reason. There are *two* gaps between the 3-point and the 6-point, so the 3-point doesn't form as effective a block:

Diagram 23. Black has played 5-3

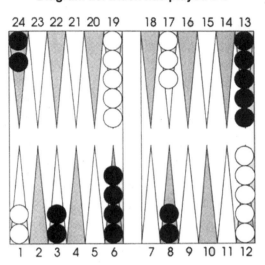

Still, the 3-point is an inner board point, and there's no better way to play this roll.

6-1: Make the bar-point (7-point)

This roll is a little stronger than a 5-3, about on a par with a 4-2.

Diagram 24. Black has played 6-1

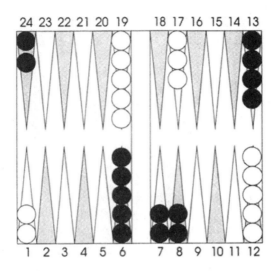

By making the *bar-point*, Black has succeeded in creating a block three points long. In backgammon, long blocks of consecutive points are called **primes**, and one key goal is to build a prime and trap your opponent's men behind it. With the 6-1 roll, Black is well on his way to making a prime. The only drawback to this roll is that the 7-point is not an inner-board point, so it doesn't help keep White from entering if you send him to the bar.

6-5 LOVER'S LEAP:
Play From Your 24-Point to the Midpoint

6-5 is a special roll, since it's the only number that lets you get a back checker all the way to the security of your midpoint (the 13-point). This is a good roll, although not quite as good as starting with a point-making throw.

Diagram 25. Black has played 65

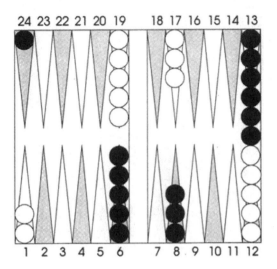

THE BAR-POINT SPLIT PLAYS:
6-2, 6-3, and 6-4

Now we're going to look at rolls that can't be played by simply making new points. These rolls require a little more creativity and imagination. We're going to play these rolls the same way.

Diagram 26. Black has played 6-2

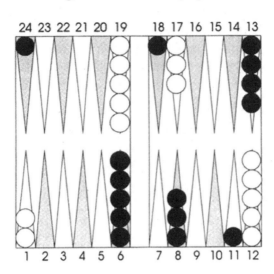

6-2

As you see, we recommend a very bold play with 6-2: one checker from the 24-point to the 18-point, and one checker from the 13-point to the 11-point. Black opens up three blots around the board. Why?

In the answer lies the essence of dynamic backgammon: Black has no way to play this number safely, so instead he's placing his checkers directly on the points he *wants* to make. In effect, he's challenging White to a fight: "Hit me if you can, he's saying, "but in return I may just hit you back."

Black can gain from this play in two ways: White might throw a poor number next turn and miss Black's blots altogether. Although White can hit with sixes and ones, he misses with twos, threes, fours, and fives. So it's by no means certain that he can hit at all. Even if he does hit, he'll probably have to leave blots of his own. Then Black might enter from the bar and hit those blots. An exchange of hits like that could leave Black well ahead in the race.

Of course, White might roll perfectly. For instance, he might roll a 6-1 and make the 18-point with checkers from the 12-point and the 17-point, sending your checker to the bar to boot! That's a risk you take when you play dynamically. You give your opponent a few chances to smash you with great rolls, while in return you have a good chance to make substantial progress.

6-3, 6-4
With 6-3 and 6-4, you should make similar plays. With 6-3, play one checker from the 24-point to the 18-point, and another from the 13-point to the 10-point. With 6-4, play one checker from the 24-point to the 18-point and one from the 13-point to the 9-point.

Diagram 27. Black has played 6-4

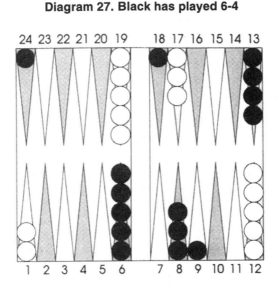

The alert reader will have noticed that Black had another play with 6-4: he could have made an inner board point by playing from the 8-point to the 2-point and from the 6-point to the 2-point. Why did we reject this play?

To see why, take a look again at our comments to the 5-3 play. We pointed out there that the gaps between the 3-point and the 6-point made a formation that was not so effective for blocking. The same is true for making the 2-point, only more so. The 2-point is so far from the 6-point and 8-point that it has little, if any, blocking value.

This leads to another rule of thumb in backgammon: *beware of making your 1-point and 2-point early in the game.* Checkers on these points are away from the main scene of the action, and can easily become liabilities instead of assets.

THE BUILDING PLAYS:
5-4, 4-3, 5-2, and 3-2.

I like to call these rolls the **building plays**. Except for **5-4**, all of these rolls could be played completely safely. With **4-3** and **5-2**, Black could play a checker all the way from the 13-point to the 6-point. With **3-2**, Black could play from the 13-point to the 8-point. In many parts of the world, or among groups of beginners, it's not uncommon to see these rolls played in just that fashion.

But that's not the dynamic way–the winning way. I prefer to use the rolls to prepare to make good points next turn. If my opponent can throw a perfect shot and hit me, more power to him. I won't be out of the game. But if I get away with these plays, I'll be building up my position quickly. That's the way I like to play–full steam ahead.

Let's look at the best way to play these rolls.

5-4: Play 24-point to 20-point, and 13-point to 8-point.
My play of the **5-4** gets me ready to make an anchor on the **20-point** next turn:

Diagram 28. Black has played 5-4

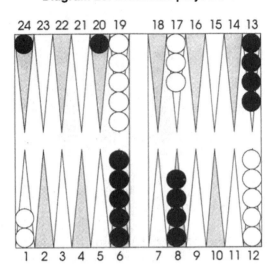

4-3: Play 24-point to 20-point, and 13-point to 10-point.

I love this roll. It leaves three blots, but I have plenty of possibilities next turn. Playing 24 to 20 prepares to make the anchor on the **20-point**, while 13 to 10 gives me many combinations to make the 4-point or the 5-point.

Diagram 29. Black has played 4-3

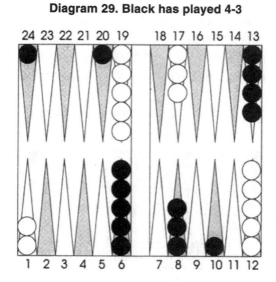

3-2: Play 13-point to 10-point, and 13-point to 11-point.

Another roll which takes a small risk for some real building potential down the road:

Diagram 30. Black has played 3-2

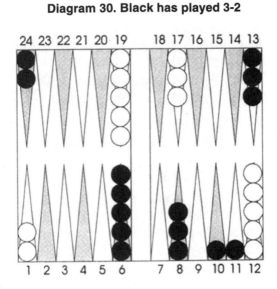

It's not so easy for White to hit those two blots, while almost all of Black's rolls will make a new point next turn. (Try them and see.)

5-2: Play 13-point to 8-point, and 13-point to 11-point.
This is the least effective of the building plays:

Diagram 31. Black has played 5-2

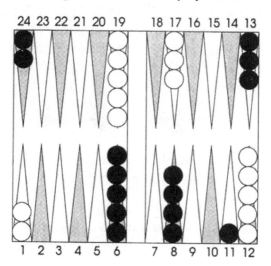

Black takes a small extra risk this turn for a few more possibilities next turn.

THE SLOTTING ROLLS:
2-1, 4-1, and 5-1.

With these plays, I advocate a really aggressive play: use the larger number to pull a man off the 13-point, and with the ace, slot the 5-point! **Slotting** means placing a blot where your opponent can hit it with a single number– in this case a 4. For instance, I play an opening 2-1 like this:

Diagram 32. Black has played a 2-1

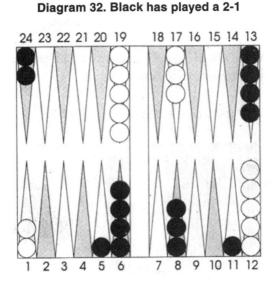

At first glance, this looks crazy. I've put a blot where my opponent can hit it with a 4, and if he hits it, I lose a lot of ground in the race to get my checkers around the board. Why would I take such a risk?

Basically, for two reasons. First of all, if my blot isn't hit, I have a great chance to cover it next turn. When I do that, it's as though I started with the best roll of all, a 3-1. Second, being hit and sent back isn't the end of the game. I can still reenter, build a defensive position, and hope to hit a **shot,** an opportunity to hit a blot, as my opponent comes around the board.

The more you play backgammon, the more you'll learn that it's very difficult to avoid leaving **shots** for the whole game. And a player whose whole game is built around playing safe will rarely be a big winner.

Here's a secret that very few beginners understand: *in backgammon, taking calculated risks isn't really risky— in the long run, it's actually the percentage play.*

That's it. Those are all the rolls that you can start the game with, and the dynamic way of playing them. You can play these openings with confidence. When you run up against a player who likes to play completely safe, piling his checkers up on the points he already owns, don't worry. He may look askance at your bold style of play, but in the long run, you'll win his money.

SAMPLE GAME 1°

The best way to see how backgammon should be played is to take a look at some actual games. You'll get a feel for what a game looks like, from start to finish, and we'll introduce some sound principles of play as we go along. We've also included plenty of diagrams, so you won't get lost along the way.

If you have a backgammon board, take it out now and set it up as we showed back in Diagram 2–the starting position. Then follow along with the game.

Be sure to take the time to actually make the moves on your board –you'll find that this greatly enhances your understanding.

In our first game, the White pieces are conducted by a player of the old school–conservative and cautious. Black is a player who understands the new dynamic style.

1. Black rolls 4-3: plays 24-point to 20-point and 13-point to 10-point.

Diagram 33. Black has played 4-3

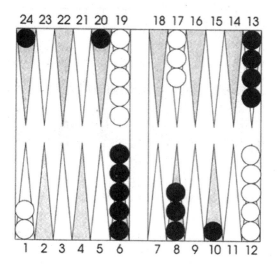

Excellent! Black didn't roll one of his best numbers, but he still made the most of his roll. By playing 24 to 20, Black stakes a claim on the 20-point, one of the most valuable points on the board. If White doesn't do anything, Black will hope to roll a 4 and make this point next turn. In addition, the checker on the 20-point now looks out over White's entire outerboard (the points from the 18-point to the 13-point). If White tries to leave a blot in this area, Black will have good chances to hit it.

The checker on the 10-point is also usefully placed, increasing the chances that Black will be able to make a blocking point next turn. Take a look: If Black's next roll is a 6-4 or a 6-2, he will be able to make the 4-point. If he rolls a 5-1 or a 5-3, he can make the 5-point. And if he rolls a 6-3, he can make the bar (7)-point. That's five new rolls that play effectively next turn because Black took a small risk this turn. That's dynamic backgammon: small risks now to earn big rewards later.

2. White rolls 4-1: Plays 12-point to 16-point and 16-point to 17-point

Diagram 34. White has played 4-1

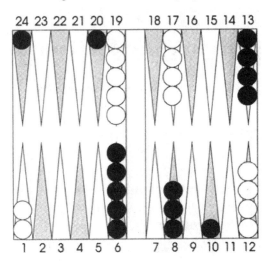

White, on the other hand, plays very conservatively. While his play is perfectly safe (it leaves no blots), it's also completely unconstructive–White is no closer to building a new point or escaping his back men than he was at the beginning of the game.

Did White have a better play? I think so. In his position, I would have made this play–19-point to 20-point, hitting Black's blot, and 1-point to 5-point. Take a look at how this move looks:

Diagram 35. White has played 4-1 the recommended way

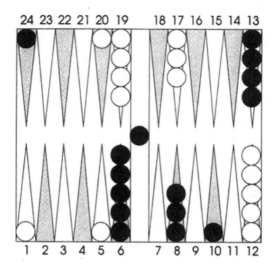

See the difference? White is now attacking both 5-points: Black's (the 5-point) and White's (the 20-point). In addition, Black is on the bar, and will have to enter that checker before he can do anything else. Sure, Black may be able to enter and hit White somewhere. But if he doesn't, he's in serious trouble, and even if he does, so what? The game is just getting started and there's a lot of play to come. At least this way, White has made some progress toward a couple of his goals. Next turn, he might be able to make the 5-point, the 20-point, or both.

Now go back to the position in Diagram 34, and we'll look at Black's next roll in the actual game.

3. Black rolls 3-1: Plays 8-point to 5-point and 6-point to 5-point, *making* the 5-point.

Diagram 36. Position after Black plays 3-1

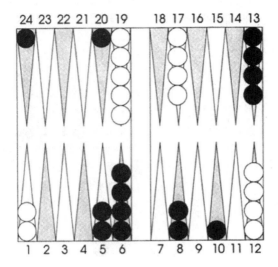

A nice roll, although notice that Black had many nice rolls in this position. That's another advantage of Black's dynamic style of play: it creates positions where a lot of rolls play well. When you play in this style, your opponents may complain about how lucky you are. Let them. You concentrate on winning.

Black's roll was so good that you may have noticed that there were a couple of other useful points that he could have made. For instance, he could have used his roll of 3-1 to make the 7-point (with the checkers on the 8-point and 10-point) or the 20-point (by moving up the checker on the 24-point). Why did he pick the 5-point instead of one of these other plays?

Let's take the possibilities one by one. He picked the 5-point over the 7-point because, although both are blocking points, the 5-point is also an *inner*-board point. That means it will help keep White on the bar if Black can score a hit. He picked the 5-point over the 20-point because he feels it will be relatively easy to make the 20-point next turn, or, if need be, to run the checker from the 20-point over to Black's **outfield** (in the area of the 9, 10 and 11-points).

The 5-point, on the other hand, might be hard to make, since Black only has a few throws each turn which can make it. In this case, with two possible goals, Black chose to make the one that was *harder* to do, leaving the relatively easy one for later. That's a good rule to remember.

4. White rolls 5-4: Plays 12-point to 17-point and 12-point to 16-point.

Diagram 37. White has played 5-4

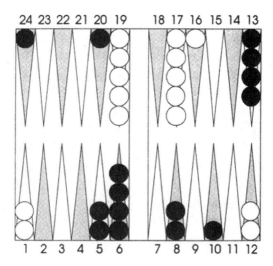

A bad roll for White, which forces him to leave a blot somewhere. His play is all right, although playing 12-point to 21-point was also OK.

5. Black rolls 6-4: Plays 20-point to 16-point, hitting White's blot, and continues on to the 10-point.

Diagram 38. Black has played 6-4, hitting

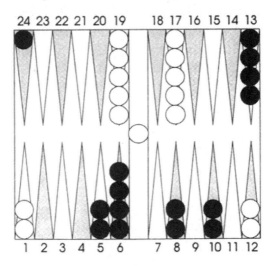

A great shot for Black, which accomplishes three objectives at once: hitting White, escaping one of his back checkers, and making a new point. It's hard to do more with a single roll. White's passive play has led him into serious difficulties.

6. White rolls 3-1: Plays bar to 3-point, and continues on to the 4-point.

Diagram 39. White has played 3-1 from the bar

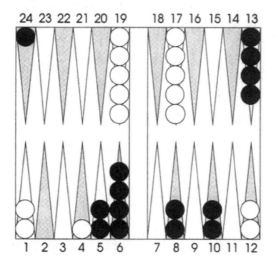

Remember that when you have a checker on the bar, you *must* reenter that checker before you can move any other checker. Since White rolled 3-1, the first half of his move had to be one of two plays: either use the 1 to enter, by playing bar to 1-point, or use the 3 to enter, by playing bar to 3-point. White chose the latter. That left him with a 1 to play, which he decided to play with the checker he had just entered. Legally, however, he could have used this one with any of his other checkers, had he wanted to.

This roll shows the other drawback of being hit. Not only did White lose ground in the race, but he lost the opportunity to use the roll constructively. Normally, he would have used the 3-1 to make the 20-point with checkers from the 19-point and the 17-point, but here he didn't have that opportunity.

At this point, it should be clear that Black has an advantage in the game. He's built two new points, the 5-point and the 10-point; he's escaped one of his two back checkers, while White has lost ground and now has three checkers back instead of two; and he's well ahead in the race to come home. Many players might let this opportunity slip by, but not Black!

7. Instead of rolling, Black doubles to 2!
Remember what we said in the section on doubling earlier in this book. To double, Black picks up the cube, turns it to the face labelled **2**, places it on White's side of the board, and says, *I double.* (Sneering is optional.) Now it's up to White to *drop*, and concede one point, or *take*, and play on with the value of the game doubled. A game would now be worth two points, a gammon, four points, and a backgammon, six points. However, once he has accepted the cube, White cannot be doubled again. He gets to play the game out to the finish, or until the advantage swings his way and he gets to redouble Black!

DOUBLING GUIDELINES
When should you offer a double, and when should you take a double? This is one of the most difficult, perhaps *the* most difficult, decision in backgammon. Doubling and taking doubles requires tremendous judgement and experience, and you'll find that the longer you play the game, the more your knowledge of doubling deepens and expands. But here are a few guidelines:

• You should be willing to take a double if you have at least a 25% chance of winning the game, and you're unlikely to lose a gammon or a backgammon. This fact comes as a surprise to many people, since at first it seems that you wouldn't want to take a double if you're an underdog. Why play for more if you can just give the game up? But that's not the right way to look at the situation.

• To see where the 25% number comes from, consider this example: suppose you were in a position that you knew you could win just one time in four. Suppose you sat down to play this position four times against another player, and he started each game by doubling you. Here's what could happen:

If you dropped each of the four doubles, you would lose four games at one point per game. Net loss: four points.

If you took each of the four doubles, you would lose three games and win one. At two points per game, you would lose six points in the three games you lost, and win two points in the one game you won. Net loss: four points—exactly the same as if you dropped!

That's why 25% is the break-even point for accepting doubles. If you have a better chance than that, you should take, and with worse chances, you drop.

• How big a favorite should you be to double? That's a good question, and there's a lot of disagreement about this question, even among the best players. (That's part of what makes backgammon such an interesting and exciting game–there's so much that isn't yet understood, even among the acknowledged grandmasters.) Most players feel that the side contemplating a double should be at least be a 2-1 favorite, or even a little better. Aggressive players like to double a little earlier than this, while some conservative players try to get very close to the 75% mark before doubling.

Now let's get back to our game. We listed Black's advantages a little while ago. Black feels that the sum total of these advantages makes him at least a 2-1 favorite to win the game, so he doubles. What should White do?

8. White Accepts the Double
White decides that he can win this position at least 25% of the time, so he takes the double. Why did he think that? Answer–he guessed, based upon his experience in playing positions of this sort. As you play backgammon, you will build up experience and make your own decisions about the strength of certain formations. There are no cut-and-dried formulas for deciding questions of this sort. Players just make their own best judgments.

Was White correct? I don't think so. Although Black's game is not yet overwhelmingly strong, White has as yet nothing going for him. I think it's too hard for White to turn the game around quickly, and I like to give up such positions. Still, many reasonable players might disagree with this assessment. At any rate, White's take means we have an interesting game ahead of us.

9. Black rolls 6-2: Plays 10-point to 4-point, hitting, and 6-point to 4-point.

Diagram 40. Black has played 6-2

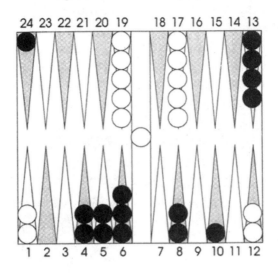

Black's second great shot in a row. Now White is really in trouble. There is no disagreement on how to play this roll. Any time you can make an inner-board point and hit your opponent at the same time, you should do so.

10. White rolls 2-2: Plays bar to 2-point, 17-point to 21-point, and 19-point to 21-point.

Diagram 41. White has played 2-2

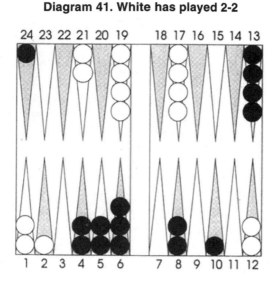

White finally builds an inner-board point, which was a long time coming. In part, this was a result of White's ultra-conservative opening strategy. It's difficult to build points without being willing to take some risks in the opening.

Although this was a good roll by White, it doesn't change the fact that Black has a very big advantage. In fact, if Black were to double in this position, White would have a mandatory pass.

11. Black Rolls 5-4: Plays 24-point to 15-point.

Diagram 42. Black has played 5-4

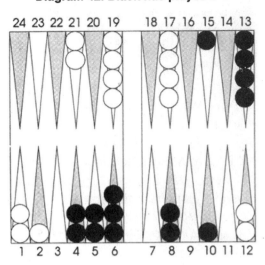

Not an especially good roll. Black would have liked a 6-4, which he would have played 8-point to 2-point and 6-point to 2-point, making a point *on White's head,* or perhaps a 6-3, which he would have played 13-point to 7-point and 10-point to 7-point, making a *5-point prime.* His roll of 5-4 is not completely useless, however. By running to the 15-point, he is preparing to escape his last checker.

DUPLICATION STRATEGY

This play also illustrates a principle known as **duplication**. Here's how it works. White would like to hit one of the two Black blots in the position. The Black checker on the 15-point can be hit by the White checkers on the 12-point, but White needs to throw a 3 on one die or the other to hit.

Now look at the Black checker on the 10-point. That can be hit by the White checkers on the 1-point and 2-point, but only if White throws a particular combination of numbers. The only combinations that will work are 6-3 (to hit from the 1-point) and 5-3 (to hit from the 2-point). Notice that these two rolls both contain a 3, the same number that White needed to hit from the 12-point.

In backgammon parlance, we say that *White's 3s are duplicated.* He needs the same number to hit on one side of the board as the other, which ensures that most of White's dice combinations (all those that don't contain a 3 on either die) *won't* hit. That's good news for Black, bad news for White.

If, while playing a game, you can duplicate your opponent's good numbers as much as possible, you'll ensure that he has fewer useful numbers to play. In the long run, that means more winning games for you, and fewer for him.

12. White rolls 6-4: Plays 17-point to 23-point and 19-point to 23-point.

Diagram 43. White has played 6-4

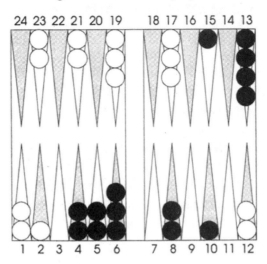

White misses his shot, but is able to build another point in his inner board. However, this was a costly miss. Black has now escaped his last rear checker, one of the key goals of successful strategy. Black's also far ahead in the race, so to win, White will have to hit a last-ditch shot as Black brings his men home.

The next few moves should be a period of consolidation. Black will try to bring his men home safely, hopefully making his 3-point and 7-point in the process. White will fill in the gaps in his own home board, hoping to hit a shot much later in the game.

13. Black rolls 6-3: Plays 13-point to 7-point and 10-point to 7-point.

Diagram 44. Black has played 6-3

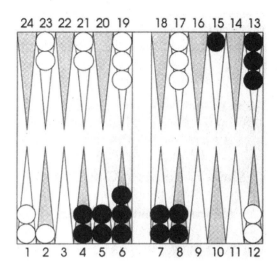

An excellent play by Black. Notice that this is not the safest play. Black could have played 15-point to 6-point, or 15-point to 9-point and 13-point to 10-point, either of which would have left White fewer chances to hit a Black blot than the play he made.

Black was willing to leave White a direct shot at his checker on the 15-point because he understands the tremendous power of the five-point block (or prime) that he created with his play. Suppose that White hits the blot on the 15-point next urn. How is the game likely to go from that point? Black will soon reenter his checker on White's inner board. White may be able to hit again, but Black will quickly escape.

Meanwhile, White's three checkers on the 1-point and 2-point are stuck. White will need to roll some aces and deuces to reach the 3-point, then several sixes to jump over the five-point prime. It's not very likely that this will happen, so Black feels that the risk that White will roll a three, hit him, and somehow win from that point is justified.

14. White Rolls 55: Plays 12-point to 22-point with two men.

Diagram 45. White has played 5-5

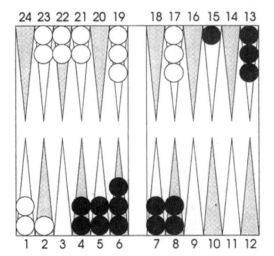

To the novice, this might look like a good roll. White advances 20 pips in the race and makes an inner board point besides. In fact, it's a poor roll, not just because White missed the blot on the 15-point, but because White is advancing too quickly.

But you ask, "If backgammon is basically a racing game, how can anyone be advancing too quickly? The faster, the better, right?" Not quite. Backgammon is much complex than just a simple racing game. That's part of what makes it so fascinating.

Here's what I mean: if both sides had broken all contact between their checkers, and were just racing home with their men, then big rolls would always be better than small rolls.

But if one side is trapped, as White is in this position, and is waiting for the chance to hit a shot later in the game, then he wants to roll small numbers at this stage of the game. He wants to make up the points in his board gradually, so that his home board is fully made up *just as he hits the shot he is waiting for. Then*, he can keep the checker he hit on the bar while he brings the remainder of his men around to join them.

If he moves too quickly at this stage of the game, his board will form and then disintegrate *before* he hits a shot, and he will lose anyway. (In fact, we'll see that very scenario happen in this game.)

15. Black rolls 6-4: Plays 15-point to 9-point, 13-point to 9-point.

Diagram 46. Black has played 6-4

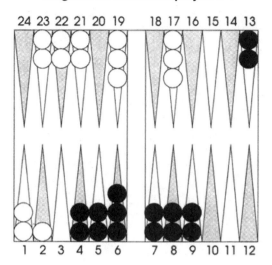

Notice that Black could have used this roll to make the 2-point (8-point to 2-point and 6-point to 2-point) but this play is much stronger. He has now completed a full 6-point prime, one of the chief goals of middle game strategy.

Notice that no matter what numbers White rolls, there is no way his men on the 1-point and 2-point can escape Black's blockade *so long as Black's prime remains intact*. Since the largest number on a die is six, there's no roll that will hop over a 6-point prime. White is trapped for the time being.

Does this mean White has no chance to win?

No, although his chances are now quite small. Since Black has to bring all his men into the home board in order to bear off, he will have to break up his prime in the near future. This process is called *rolling the prime home*, and how well Black performs this task affects his winning chances substantially.

16. White rolls 4-3: Plays 17-point to 20-point and 17-point to 21-point.

Diagram 47. White has played 4-3

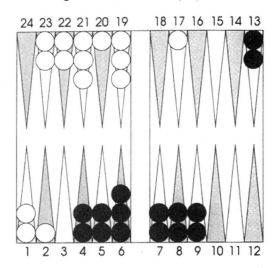

A straightforward play. White hopes to roll a 1 or a 3 next turn and make the 20-point, giving him a very strong home board.

17. Black rolls 6-2: Plays 13-point to 5-point.

Diagram 48. Black has played 6-2

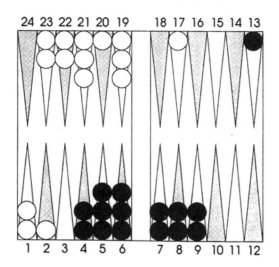

Another straightforward play. Black's next goal is to make the 3-point, if necessary giving up the 9-point in the process. If he makes the 3-point, he will have a full six-point prime from the 3-point to the 8-point, so the 9-point will be superfluous.

18. White rolls 5-3: Plays 17-point to 20-point, and 19-point to 24-point.

Diagram 49. White has played 5-3

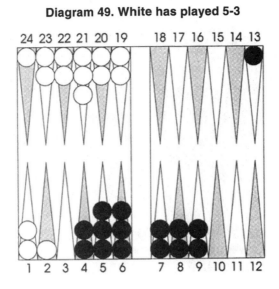

White has achieved a strong home board. If Black didn't have a prime, and White were in position to hit a blot, his home board might easily keep that checker trapped long enough for White to win. Unfortunately, there's no blot to be seen, and White's board will not last long.

19. Black rolls 6-3: Plays 9-point to 3-point and 6-point to 3-point.

Diagram 50. Black has played 6-3

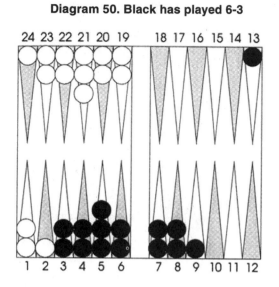

A great shot. Black *rolls his prime* forward one pip. Black's blot on the 9-point is quite safe, as there are no sevens on the dice!

20. White rolls 5-4: Plays 19-point to 24-point and 19-point to 23-point.

Diagram 51. White has played 5-4

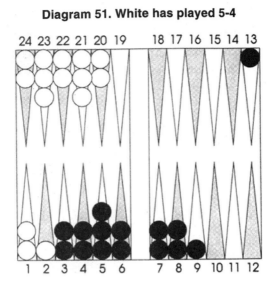

There goes the neighborhood as Billy Horan (one of backgammon's strongest grandmasters) is fond of saying.

21. Black rolls 3-2: Plays 9-point to 7-point and 5-point to 2-point, hitting.

Diagram 52. Black has played 3-2

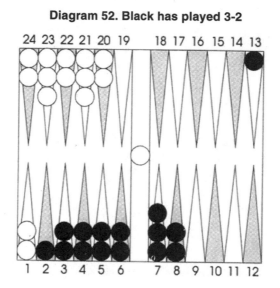

Black hits, even though White could roll a two and hit him right back. Bold play? Not at all. Since Black has a full 6-point prime, White can never escape. It may take Black some time to enter a checker from the bar if he is hit, but it won't matter, since his prime cannot break while he is on the bar.

22. White rolls 5-4: No play.
White can't move, since Black owns both the 5-point and the 4-point. Remember that if you are on the bar, you must enter the checker before you can move any other checkers. In this case, White needed to roll either a one or a two on the dice to enter, since those are the only open points in Black's home board.

23. Black rolls 6-6: Plays 13-point to 7-point, and 8-point to 2-point with two men. Cannot play fourth six.

Diagram 53. Black has played 6-6

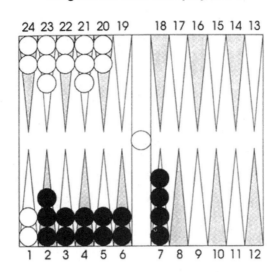

When you roll a double, you get to play that number four times, *if possible*. In this case, Black has only three legal plays of a six. The checkers on the 7-point cannot move six pips, because White owns the 1-point. In backgammon lingo, his sixes are *killed*.

24. White rolls 4-1: Plays bar to 1-point, and 20-point to 24-point.

Diagram 54. White has played 4-1

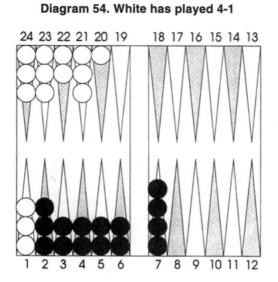

A forced play. White has managed to enter from the bar, but loses another home board point in the process.

25. Black rolls 4-3: Plays 7-point to 3-point, and 7-point to 4-point.

Diagram 55. Black has played 4-3

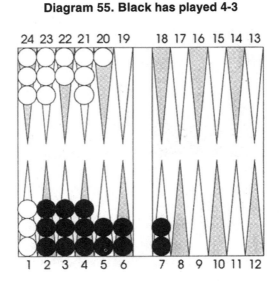

Remember that Black can't bear off any men until *all* his checkers are in the home board (points 1 through 6). His last task before the bearoff is to bring the four checkers on the 7-point into his home board somewhere. With this roll, he brings in two of the checkers.

26. White rolls 5-3: Plays 20-point to 23-point with the 3; cannot play a 5.

Diagram 56. White has played 5-3

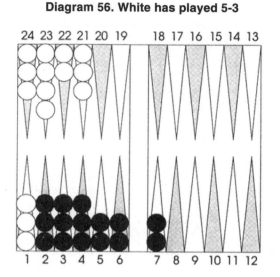

White has no legal way to play a 5, since his checkers on the 1-point are blocked, and there are no checkers on the other side of the board that can move five spaces. In that case, he only has to play a 3, which he does.

27. Black rolls 5-5: Plays two checkers from 7-point to 2-point, then bears off two checkers from the 5-point.

Diagram 57. Black has played 5-5

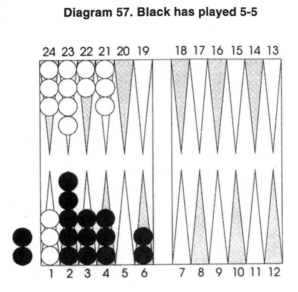

Black plays his first two fives from the 7-point to the 2-point. Once he has done this, he has all 15 checkers in the inner board, so he is entitled to start bearing off checkers. With his two remaining fives, he removes the two checkers on his 5-point.

28. White rolls 6-2: Plays 1-point to 9-point.

Diagram 58. White has played 6-2

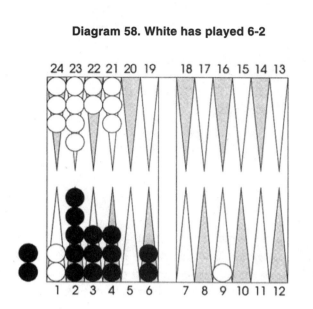

Now that Black has **broken** his 7-point, White is once again free to move sixes.

29. Black rolls 6-5: Bears off a checker from the 6-point; no legal 5 to play.

Diagram 59. Black has played 6-5

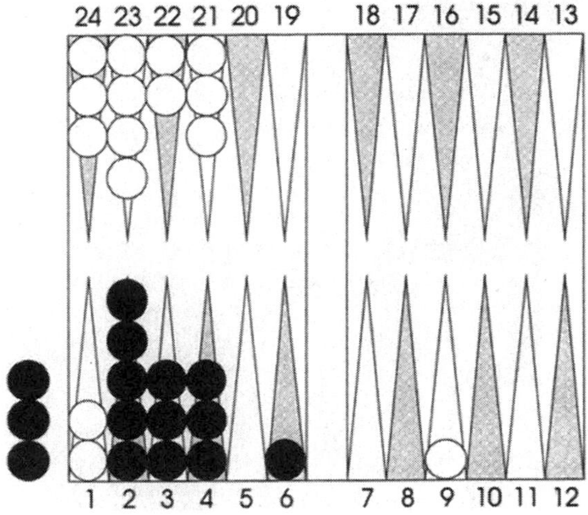

Look at this position carefully to make sure you understand what has happened. Black used the six to bear off
one of his checkers from the 6-point. He would normally
use the 5 to bear off a checker from the 5-point, but there
are no more checkers on the 5-point. If White didn't still
own the 1-point, Black could use his 5 to play 6-point to
1-point, but that's impossible here. So Black has no way
to play the 5, and gives up that part of his roll.

30. White rolls 3-2: Pays 9-point to 14-point.

Diagram 60. White has played 3-2

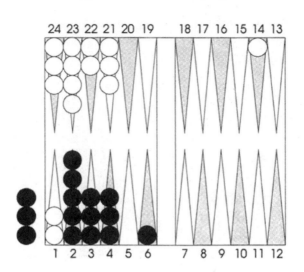

Too bad! White had some winning chances if he could have hit Black's blot by throwing any number containing a 5, or the combination number 4-1. As is, he has nothing better than to bring his checker in the outfield closer to home.

31. Black rolls 6-5: Bears off a checker from the 6-point and a checker from the 4-point.

Diagram 61. Black has played 6-5

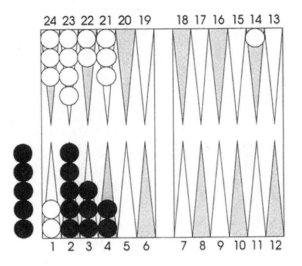

Look at this play closely and compare it to Black's last play. These situations cause some confusion for new-comers to the game. This turn, Black uses the 6 to bear a checker off the 6-point, as you might expect. Then, since Black has a 5 left to play and no checkers on the 5-point or 6-point he is able to use the 5 to bear off from the next highest point, in this case the 4-point.

Why couldn't he bear off from the 4-point last turn (move 29)? Because in that case he still had a checker on a point higher than the 4-point. *You can only bear off from a point with a higher number than the point itself if all the higher points have been cleared of checkers.* Study these two examples carefully, and you'll avoid any confusion at the table.

32. White rolls 3-2: Plays 14-point to 19-point.

Diagram 62. White has played 3-2

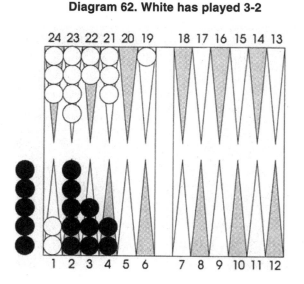

White is piddling along. Not only is he very unlikely to win the game, but there is now a real possibility that he could lose a gammon. Remember, if your opponent bears *all* his men off before you bear off *any* men, you lose a gammon, or twice the value of the doubling cube. Since the cube is now on 2, White will lose four points if he loses a gammon!

33. Black rolls 6-2: Bears off a checker from the 4-point, and plays 4-point to 2-point.

Diagram 63. Black has played 6-2

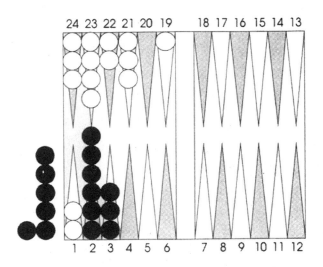

Since Black has no checkers on the 5-point or the 6-point, he can use any 4, 5, or 6 on the dice to bear off from the 4-point.

You may ask, "Why didn't he take two men off, by using the 2 to bear off from the 2-point?" That would have been perfectly legal. However, it would have left a vulnerable blot on the 4-point, which White could then have hit if he rolled any 3. Black avoided this possibility by **picking up** the blot on the 4-point.

34. White rolls 4-3: Plays 1-point to 8-point.

Diagram 64. White has played 4-3

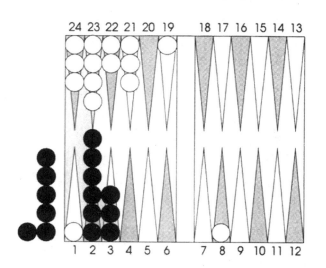

White has little choice on his moves any longer. He must start running his back checkers out to try to avoid losing a gammon.

Why not move both back men, by playing 1-point to 5-point and 1-point to 4-point?

Because White still has chances of hitting one of Black's blots, which would still give him some chances of winning the game. If Black's next roll is 6-5, for example, he will have to bear two men off the 3-point, leaving a blot there which White could hit.

If you take a look at Black's position, you will find that almost half his numbers leave a shot next turn. (Count them!)

35. Black rolls 6-1: Bears a checker off the 3-point with the six, and plays 2-point to 1-point, hitting White.

Diagram 65. Black has played 6-1

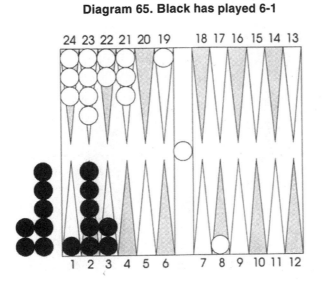

Black had to leave another shot (his only other legal play with the ace was to play 3-point to 2-point), so he made the most aggressive play, putting White on the bar.

36. White rolls 4-2: Plays bar to 4-point and continues on to the 6-point.

Diagram 66. White has played 4-2

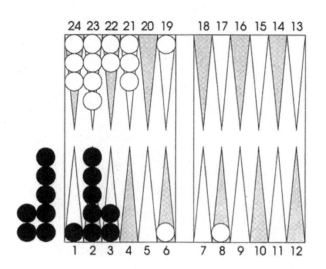

White's winning chances are now gone. There's no way he can win the race, now matter how well he rolls or how poorly Black rolls. But we continue playing, because it's not decided whether Black will win a single game (worth 2 points) or a gammon (worth 4 points).

37. Black rolls 2-2: Bears four men off the 2-point.

Diagram 67. Black has played 2-2

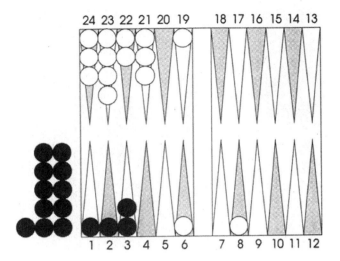

A great roll for Black, and now the gammon looks quite likely.

38. White rolls 5-1: Plays 8-point to 13-point, and 6-point to 7-point.

Diagram 68. White has played 5-1

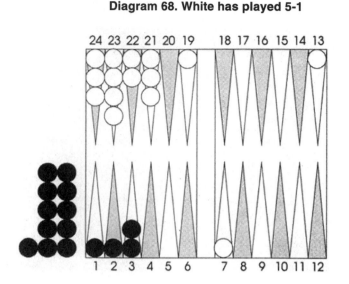

Take a look at that ace that White just played. It may look insignificant, but that accurate play might have saved White two more points!

Remember what we said before in our chapter about the rules–if one side bears off all its checkers while the other side has no checkers off and at least one checker in the other side's home board, that's a triple game, or backgammon. With the cube on two, a backgammon is worth six points!

So by moving that last checker out of Black's inner board, White has avoided the possibility of losing a triple game.

39. Black rolls 6-3: Bears off two men from the 3-point.

Diagram 69. Black has played 6-3

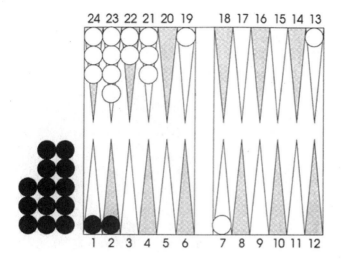

24 23 22 21 20 19   18 17 16 15 14 13

1 2 3 4 5 6   7 8 9 10 11 12

Forced play.

40. White rolls 4-4: Plays 7-point to 19-point with three fours, and 13-point to 17-point with the last four.

Diagram 70. White has played 4-4

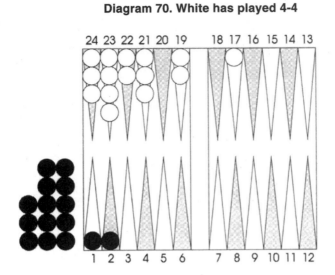

That last roll moved a lot of freight, but not quite enough to save the gammon.

In the final position, Black doesn't even have to roll. Even his smallest number (2-1) will bear off his last two checkers, so he just claims a gammon, and writes **plus-4** on the scoresheet.

There's our first look at a real backgammon game. Play through it two or three times for practice. You'll find that your knowledge of the backgammon rules is greatly strengthened. Also, some of the plays in the game, which may have looked strange at first glance, will now start to make more sense to you.

Sample Game Summary
What really happened in this game? Black made several

dynamic plays in the early game, and White responded passively. As Black's plan came to fruition, White found himself trapped in what is known as an **ace-point game**– a position in which one player is trapped on their opponent's ace-point, hoping to hit a shot in the late stages of the game.

As you play backgammon, you'll see a fair number of ace-point games, and you'll eventually learn to play them properly from either side.

Now let's move on and look at a completely different type of game.

SAMPLE GAME 2: THE BLITZ!

Up to now, we've described moves in a pretty lengthy fashion, so as to be crystal clear. In most books, backgammon moves aren't described this way, because it takes up too much space and is clumsy to read. Instead, games are recorded in **backgammon notation**. It was first invented by Paul Magriel, one of backgammon's greatest players and writers, back in the 1970s.

Here's how backgammon notation works:

· Instead of saying **Black rolls 3-2,** we'll just write Black 32.

• Instead of saying **13-point to 10-point**, we'll write 13/10.

• If an opposing blot is hit, we put an asterisk after the play, like this: **12/6***.

• If two men move from one point to another, we'll say this: **20/16(2)**.

• If a checker enters from the bar, we'll write **Bar/20**.

• And if a player bears off a checker, we'll write **3/off**.

The example above looks like this in standard backgammon notation: **Black 32: 13/10, 8/6*.** Quite a savings in space, and just as clear, once you get used to it. Set up your board in the initial position, and follow along.

1. White 64: 1/11
2. Black 55: 6/1*(2) 8/3(2).

Diagram 71. Black has played 55

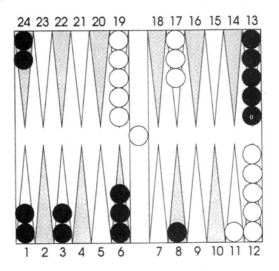

With his opening 64, White ran out to the 11-point. That wasn't our recommended play back in our chapter on dynamic openings, but it's a common way of playing the roll, and you'll see it a lot.

The Blitz
Black was hoping to hit this checker by rolling a 2, but instead he rolls a 55. To play the 55, he uses checkers from the 6-point and the 8-point to make two of his inner board points in one swoop, putting White on the bar at the

same time. This is a very aggressive way of playing double-fives, and it starts a new type of game which we haven't seen before, called the **blitz.**

In a blitz (sometimes called an **attacking game**), one side tries to close his inner board very quickly, before the opponent can establish an anchor anywhere. This game plan can only be tried if your opponent has broken the anchor he started with, back on the one-point.

As long as your opponent retains the anchor on the one-point, he has no blots for you to hit. Once he breaks that anchor, the blots he creates become vulnerable to attack.

When a blitz works, your opponent gets a checker or two trapped on the bar before he's had a chance to develop his game at all; the result is usually a gammon for you. When it fails, the other player usually gains a steady advantage, because you've moved your checkers too far forward too quickly. It's a double-edged game plan, suitable for players with an aggressive style. Let's see how it works in this game.

3. White 66: No move
With Black owning his 6-point, White is stuck on the bar and can't enter. This rolls illustrates some of the power of an early attack. White throws one of his very best numbers, which would normally make him a significant favorite in the game, and instead has to waste it completely.

4. Black: Doubles to 2
A **blitz** is a powerful game plan, and Black wastes no

time in doubling the stakes. He's already a favorite in the game.

5. White: Takes the double
White's in some trouble, but he still has plenty of chances to win. All top players would agree with this take.

6. Black 62: 13/7, 13/11*

Diagram 72. Black has played 62

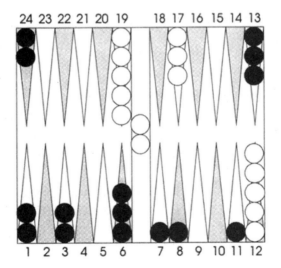

With this roll, Black's blitz is in full swing. White now has two checkers stuck on the bar, while Black has moved an impressive array of **builders** into position to make the open points in his board.

7. White 65: Bar/5
Since the 6-point is occupied, White can only enter one checker, using the 5 he rolled. This was not a good roll,

since Black can hit this checker with any combination of ones, two, threes, and sixes.

8. Black 63: 11/5*, 8/5
A good shot by Black. He uses to builders to make the 5-point *on White's head*. Black has now strengthened his 3-point board to a 4-point board, and White is in serious trouble.

Diagram 73. Black has played 63

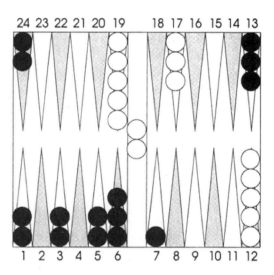

9. White 53: No move
Once again, White rolls a number that does not enter either checker from the bar, since Black has made both the 3-point and the 5-point.

10. Black 64: 13/7, 13/9

Diagram 74. Black has played 64

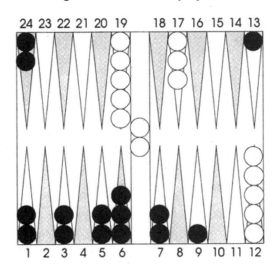

More ammunition! At this point Black is not concerned with his own back checkers. He's throwing all his energies into the blitz, trying to close out White's two checkers before White can gain a foothold. If he succeeds, he'll be able to escape his own back checkers at his leisure. If he fails, it won't matter very much whether Black shuffled his back men a little or not.

Remember the Foreman-Ali fight in Zaire? Foreman used all his energy trying to knock Ali out in the first few rounds. That's analogous to what Black is trying to do here. If Black's knockout punch fails (as did Foreman's) then the advantage will swing quickly back in the other direction.

11. White 43: Bar/4

Diagram 75. White has played 43

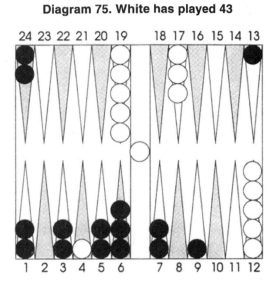

White was hoping to throw fours or twos. He threw a single four, which enabled him to enter one of his two men.

12. Black 54: 9/4* 13/9

Diagram 76. Black has played 54

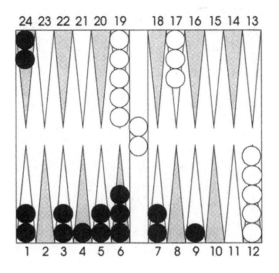

Black had another choice here. He could have made his 2-point, by playing 7/2, 6/2. Many players would have chosen that move, which gives Black a five-point inner board. However, if White then throws *any* four, he has his anchor and the security that it offers.

Black is trying as hard as he can to prevent White from ever making any anchor at all. With that in mind, he aims to hit any White checker that lands in his board. It's all or nothing for Black at this point.

13. White 52: Bar/2

Diagram 77. White has played 52

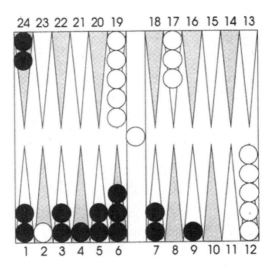

White wanted to roll a four and hit back. Black would then lose time bringing that checker in, and White would have a better chance of anchoring. But at least White was able to get one checker in. Now he has a chance to anchor if he throws a two next turn.

14. Black 52: 7/2*, 4/2

Diagram 78. Black has played 52

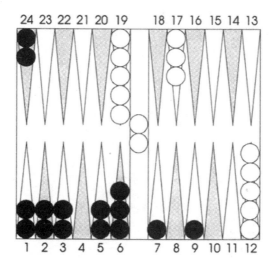

Excellent play by Black! He had a couple of chances to go wrong here. One possibility was playing something like 9/4 and 24/22. This makes a five-point board, but doesn't put White on the bar. That's too passive. White could roll a two, anchor on the 2-point, then win the game later on.

Another possibility was 6/4 and 7/2*. This makes a 5-point board and leaves White on the bar with both men, but it exposes Black to a direct return shot from the bar. If White rolls a two in response, he hits Black and slows down his attack. Black's actual play was much better. He hits White, puts two checkers up in the air, makes a 5-point board, and doesn't expose any blots to a return shot. It's the perfect combination of aggression and safety.

15. White 64: Bar/4

Diagram 79. White has played 64

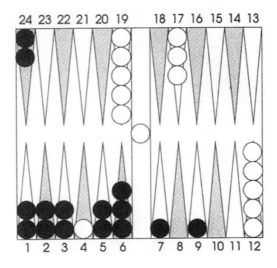

White's still fighting.

16. Black 43: 7/4*, 24/20

Diagram 80. Black has played 43

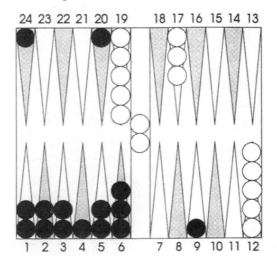

Black hits, of course, with the three. What about the four? There's no way he can improve his blitzing possibilities with the four, because he already has his only two spare checkers within range of the 4-point: the checker on the 9-point and the checker on the 6-point. Now it's time to get the back checkers moving.

17. White 54: Bar/4*

Diagram 81. White has played 54

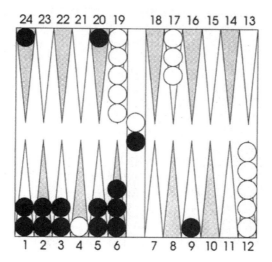

Ouch! Finally White hits a shot from the bar. Will he roll another four and put an end to Black's attack?

18. Black 64: Bar/21, 20/14

Diagram 82. Black has played 64

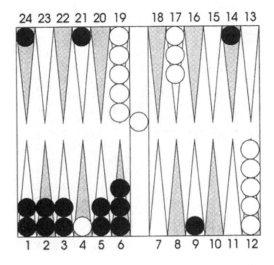

Black can't use the 6 to enter, since a 6 takes him to the 19-point, which is blocked. So Black has to enter with the 4, on the 21-point. That leaves him with a 6 to play, which he uses to move the checker from the 20-point to the 14-point. The 14-point is 10 pips away from the 4-point, so Black now can hit on the 4-point with rolls totalling 10: 6-4 and 5-5.

In fact, by moving out to the 14-point, the roll of 5-5 next turn will actually close the 4-point, assuming, of course, that White stays out.

19. White 52: Stays out. A bad shot for White.

20. Black 55: 14/4*, 9/4, 21/16.

Diagram 83. Black has played 55

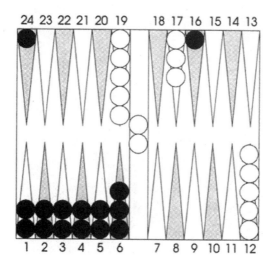

Success! With this excellent shot, Black finally succeeds in closing the board. Now Black has only a few technical problems to overcome to secure the gammon. Notice that there is no longer any need for White to roll until Black eventually opens up an inner board. With all the points 1-6 occupied, White can't enter no matter what number he rolls.

21. Black 63: 24/15

Diagram 84. Black has played 63

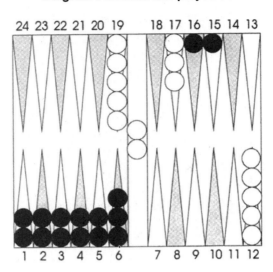

Black's correct strategy is to bring his two back men out together. He's trying to avoid being in a situation where rolling a big double (like 5-5) would cause him to open up points in his home board because his back checker is blocked. When he can move his two back men beyond White's midpoint, this possibility will disappear.

22. Black 41: 16/11

23. Black 65: 15/10, 11/5

Diagram 85. Black has played 65

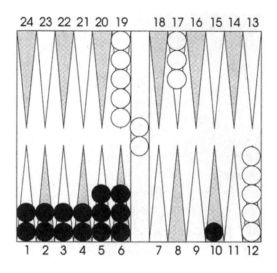

According to plan. Black has succeeded in **breaking contact**, and in a moment he will start his bearoff. If he can avoid being hit as White tries to come in, he will almost certainly win a gammon.

24. Black 52: 10/3

25. Black 61: 6/off, 5/4

Diagram 86. Black has played 61

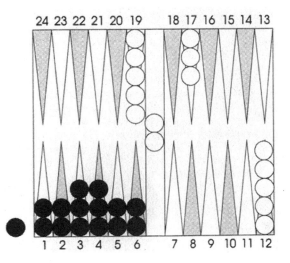

The safest way to bear off is to try and remain even on the highest points in your home board. That way, you can remove two checkers from the last point without leaving a shot. (If you had three checkers on your last point, removing just two of them would leave a costly blot.) Black's last play leaves him with two men on his 6-point, and a total of four men on his 6-point and 5-point combined. This is a safe formation.

We'll soon see an example of the danger of not remaining even on the high points.

26. Black 63: 6/off, 6/3

Diagram 87. Black has played 63

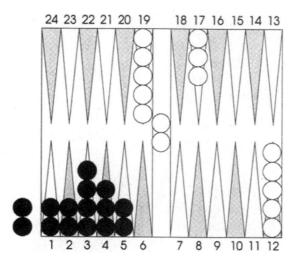

Black could take two men off by playing 6/off, 3/off, but this would leave a blot on the 6-point that White could hit by rolling a six. Instead, he correctly plays that blot to the 3-point, leaving himself safe for this turn.

Since Black has finally opened a point in his board, White gets to roll again.

27. White 54: Stays out

28. Black 65: 5/off(2)

Diagram 88. Black has played 65

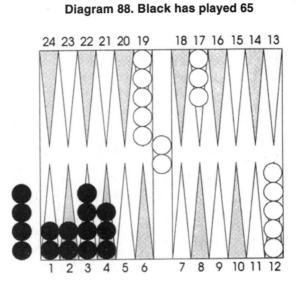

A forced play. Since Black has no checkers on the 6-point, he uses the six to bear a checker off the next highest occupied point, the 5-point. He then uses the five to bear the other checker off the 5-point.

29. White 51: Bar/5

Diagram 89. White has played 51

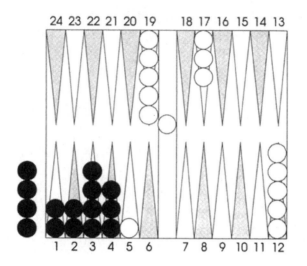

With the five, White can enter on the newly opened 5-point. The ace-point is still blocked, so he can't enter there.

30. Black 64: 4/off(2)

Diagram 90. Black has played 64

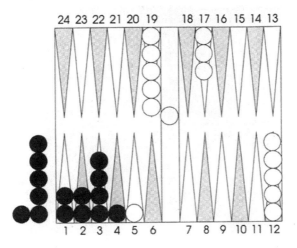

Oops! With this roll Black is forced to remove two of the three men on his 4-point. That shows why it's so important to keep an *even* number of men on the highest point when you're bearing off. Now White is back in the game if he can roll a four.

31. White 43: Bar/4*, 12/15

Diagram 91. White has played 43

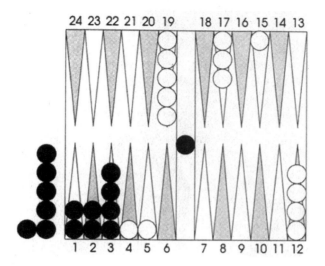

That's exciting! White hits a last-ditch shot, and now the game enters a new phase. White will try to build some points and hopefully trap the Black checker behind a blockade. If he succeeds with this plan, he'll certainly save the gammon and may even win the game.

32. Black: 55: Bar/20/15*/10/5*

Diagram 92. Black has played 55

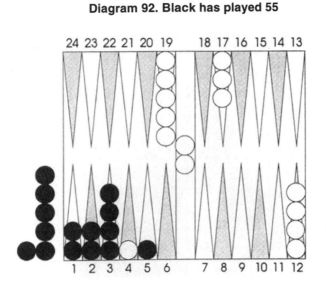

What a shot! At a backgammon tournament, this is the kind of roll that has the spectators screaming and sends the players into ecstasy or despair, depending on which side of the table you're on. Many years ago, one of backgammon's all-time great players and writers, Barclay Cooke, called backgammon "the cruelest game." It's rolls like this, just when White thought he had crept back into contention, that Cooke had in mind.

Of course, the game's not over yet. White can still roll a five and get back into contention.

33. White 61: Bar/6
Not this time. Now it looks like White really is finished.

34. Black 51: 5/4*, 4/off

Diagram 93. Black has played 51

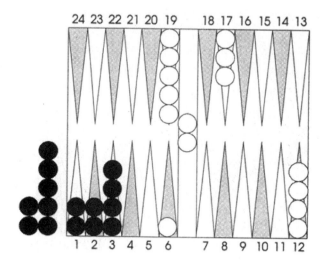

Many players would automatically play 5/off, then look around for their best ace, which would be 3/2. But Black's play is perfectly legal and considerably better. Remember that you're allowed to play your two numbers in any order, *as long as you play your entire roll.* Black has played his ace first, 5/4*, and then uses the five to bear off his checker from the 4-point, since he has no checker on a higher point. That's considered to be a legal and complete play of a five.

Why hit this checker when Black essentially has the gammon wrapped up? Black is greedy–he wants to win a backgammon worth 6 points (with the cube on 2) and not just 4 points for a gammon. Backgammon is a very seductive game (much like real life, some say) and offers many chances to be greedy, some justified, some not. You be the judge here.

35. White 53: Bar/5

36. Black 63: 3/off(2)

37. White 43: Bar/4/7

Diagram 94. White has played 43

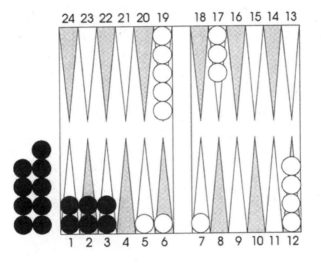

Now the outcome is settled. Even if Black throws a double next turn, nothing can prevent White from moving the men on the 5 and 6-points into Black's outer board, thus avoiding the backgammon. At the same time, there's no way Black can fail to win a gammon.

Result: four points to Black.

SAMPLE GAME 3: THE BACKGAME

In our first two sample games, one side was able to establish a quick advantage and then nurse it along to victory. Not all backgammon games proceed in such a smooth fashion. Sometimes the road to victory gets very bumpy indeed, with sudden twists and turns and wild swings of fortune. That's what gives backgammon its particular fascination, and that's what requires iron nerves to be a successful player.

Our next game is a real shootout between two very good players. These players don't shirk complications - they seek them out. It's a wild ride, typical of backgammon at its high-octane best, requiring the utmost in concentration and determination from each player. Modern backgammon isn't for the faint-of-heart: if that's the way you want to play, stick to parcheesi and canasta. If you want to see real excitement, read on.

1. Black 21: 13/11 6/5
Black starts with an innocuous throw, but he plays it as aggressively as possible - by starting his crucial 5-point and bringing down a checker from the midpoint as a backup. The 5-point is the key to modern backgammon strategy. Once you make the 5-point in the early game, you've not only doubled the strength of your home board

and started to build a prime, you've also begun the process of squeezing your opponent's back men. As Black's board gets stronger, White has to be leery about moving his back men into danger.

Not all your opponents will play this way. Some might play an opening 2-1 very conservatively, with a move like 13/11 24/23, or maybe 24/21. Those plays don't put any pressure on your game, so you'll find it easy to respond. If you run up against an opponent who plays his 2-1 like Black in this game, watch out! You're in for a real fight.

Diagram 95. Black has played 21

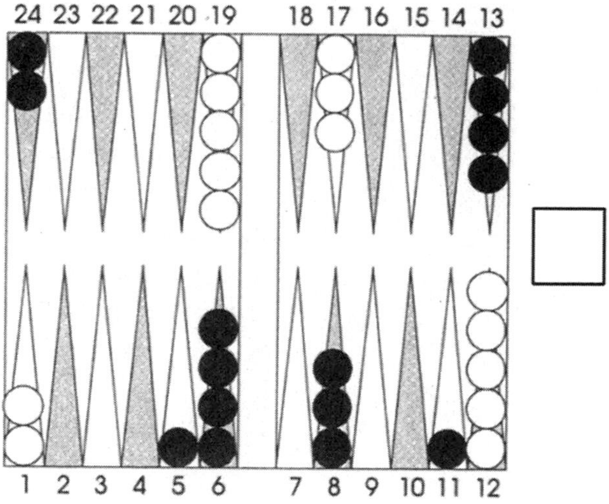

2. White 42: 1/5* 12/14
White naturally hits the blot on the 5-point, gaining in the race. With the 2, he brings a builder down to create more combinations to make a point on his side of the board.

White could play to make a point in his home board with 19/21 17/21, but this wouldn't be right. Given a choice, hitting a blot is usually stronger than making an additional point, especially if the blot has started a point in your opponent's inner board.

Diagram 96. White has played 42

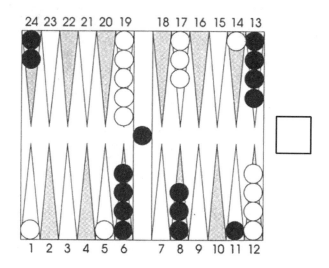

3. Black 62: Bar/23 11/5*
The struggle for Black's 5-point continues. Neither side can afford to let the other make the point uncontested. Black may fall farther behind in the race as a result of this play. However, he's not particularly concerned. Here's a good rule of thumb: *If you're well behind in the race, falling a little further behind is not a serious problem - in fact, it may well turn out to be an asset.*

4. White 52: Bar/5* 12/14
A very nice shot for White. He hits a blot, stops Black from making the 5-point, and makes the 14-point for

himself.

Diagram 97. White has played 52

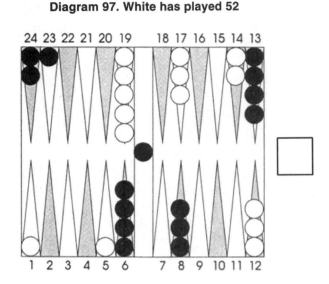

5. Black 31: Bar/22 6/5*

Black is determined to make his 5-point. Once again he enters and slashes away at the White blot. Black could play more conservatively, for instance by playing Bar/22 23/22, building a second point in White's home board.

But he doesn't - it's way too early for such a conservative play. White has still not made any new inner board points, so Black knows that even if he's hit, he'll have no trouble entering the game from the bar. Aggressive play is called for, and Black rises to the occasion.

Diagram 98. Black has played 31

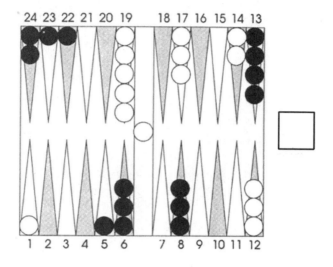

6. White 53: Bar/5* 19/22*

White hits on the 5-point, a play that's easy to understand. He also hits on the 22-point, a play that's not quite so clear.

We've learned already that the modern way of playing is to fight aggressively for your 4-point and 5-point, and to be willing to accept some loss of ground in the race in order to make those key blocking points. But here White is hitting loose on his own 3-point (labelled as the 22-point in our diagrams). Is that a good idea as well? Are all inner points worth fighting for?

The answer is - it depends.

At the beginning of the game, the 5-point is the most valuable point on the board, and well worth fighting for, as we're seeing in this game. The 4-point is not as valuable as the 5, but it's still an important point, so fights will develop over the 4-point as well. The 3-point and the 2-point are less valuable, and usually players won't waste a lot of energy fighting over those points. The 1-point definitely isn't worth fighting over - if you see a player hitting on the 1-point, it's usually with some other purpose in mind.

Perhaps he's trying to conduct a blitz, or perhaps he's under attack and needs desperately to take away part of his opponent's next roll.

Things change once points get made. If Black makes his 5-point, then his 4-point becomes the most valuable point in his board, so you can expect to see players contesting that point. If Black makes the 5-point and the 4-point, then the 3-point becomes crucial, and so on.

In the position in our game, White is hitting on the 3-point to take away Black's entire roll. Since Black has to spend his whole next roll entering from the bar, he may not be able to hit White anywhere. This could leave White free to make a new blocking point next turn. *In most positions, hitting two of your opponent's checkers is a VERY powerful play. Don't miss it!*

7. Black 64: Bar/21
One of the bonuses of hitting two checkers is that your opponent may not enter both men next turn. Here Black dances with one man, and as a result White's initiative is growing more dangerous.

Diagram 99. Black has played 64

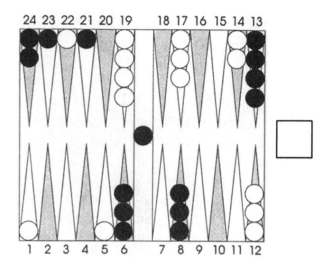

8. White Doubles to 2

White sees that the game has started very favorably for him. He's now far ahead in the race, while Black has a man still on the bar and two more vulnerable blots on the 23 and 21-points. When a good player gets the advantage, he won't usually nurse it quietly. Instead he goes straight for the throat with a quick double.

In effect he's saying to Black, "If you play this game out, my big lead could turn into a gammon or even a backgammon. Do you want to take that chance? Why risk losing four or even six points? Concede one and let's start over."

9. Black Takes the Double

An inexperienced player might be intimidated by White's threats and throw in the towel. Black, however, understands that although he is an underdog, his position has great resiliency. Falling behind in the race at the beginning of a game is not a death sentence. If Black can establish two points in White's home board, he will have what is called a "back game." White will find it difficult to bear in and bear off his checkers without leaving at least one and possibly several shots. If Black is able to hit one of these shots, he may be able to contain the checker he hits and turn the game completely around.

That's the good news. Black's plan is ambitious, however, and it can fail in several ways: White might never leave a shot, or Black might miss the shot, or Black might not be able to contain a checker even if he hits one. In that case, Black will probably lose a gammon or even a dreaded backgammon.

10. White 61: 14/20 19/20

White has several possible choices with 61. He could continue the attack with 17/23* 22/23, making the 23-point (his own 2-point) and putting a second Black checker on the bar. He could run a back man to safety with 5/12. He could make his bar-point with 12/18 17/18. Or he could make his own 5-point with the play he actually chose.

White's actual play, 14/20 19/20, is correct, strong, and completely in keeping with his strategy of aggressive, power backgammon. We've emphasized over and over again that the 5-point is the key point of modern backgammon strategy. When you make the 5-point, you crowd your opponent and prepare to build your blocking position either forward (down to the 4-point and 3-point) or backward (to the 7-point and 9-point). More than any other point on the board, the 5-point offers both immediate power and future flexibility.

However, there will always be enticing alternatives to making the 5-point. A lesser player, in the heat of battle, will allow himself to be distracted by these alternatives. If he likes playing blitzes, the play of making the 23-point might look good here. If he's had good luck in running games, the play 20/13 might be appealing. Don't let these distractions affect you! Unless another play is 100% clear, just make your 5-point.

Diagram 100. White has played 61

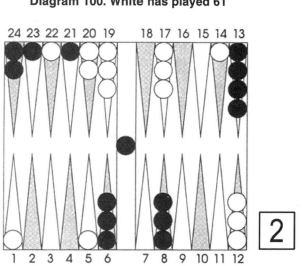

11. Black 43: Bar/21 8/5*
An excellent shot for Black. It's about time, as he's rolled poorly up to now.

Black's first decision is: Should I enter on the 22-point, hitting, or should I enter on the 21-point, making a second point? The answer is clear: **Make the second point.**

(By the way, defensive points in your opponent's home board are known as **anchors**. We'll refer to them that way from now on.)

Once Black has two anchors, he has the minimum requirements to play a back game. Here his anchors are on White's 1-point and 4-point (the 24 and 21-points in our diagrams). That formation is referred to as a "1-4 backgame."

Different backgames have different reputations. The 1-4 backgame isn't considered one of the strongest, for technical reasons which we'll get into later. The strongest back games are the 2-3, the 2-4, and the 1-3. Part of Black's strategy in this game will be to try to upgrade into a stronger back game when the opportunity presents itself.

Once Black has decided to make the 21-point, he has a 3 left to play. Here the decision is easy. He goes back to fighting for his own 5-point. If his checker is hit, so what? He already has five men back in his opponent's territory. A sixth won't matter much.

Diagram 101. Black has played 43

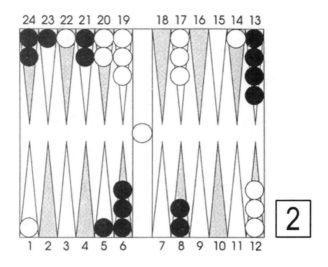

12. White 65: Bar/5*/11

White is forced to hit with the 5, of course, and then has a choice of how to play his 6. Let's look at the possibilities closely.

He could play 14/20, moving the blot on the 14-point to safety, but this is a craven play, unworthy of a modern player. White's blot on the 14-point is in a powerful spot, generating combinations to make the 18-point, the 16-point, or the 15-point, all important blocking points. White should leave the blot where it is and hope to make one of these points next turn.

White could play 12/18, directly slotting the 18-point, which both sides would like to make. This looks bold and might work, but it's really an overplay. Almost 2/3 of Black's possible numbers next turn will enter *and* hit a blot on the 18-point. Then **Black** would be a big favorite to make that key point. Here's a good rule of thumb for these situations: *If both you and your opponent want to make the same point, don't slot it! Wait to make it naturally.* In the long run, you'll make the point more often this way.

White could also slash away with 17/23*, hitting a second checker. Aggressive, but it's attacking the wrong point. White doesn't want the 23-point just yet (it's too deep in his home board. He really wants the 18-point and, to a slightly lesser extent, the 16-point. Moving that checker off the 17-point actually takes away a builder for the 18-point. Not the right idea.

By a process of elimination, we come down to 5/11 as the best choice. It creates a new builder for the important 16 and 15-points at minimal risk - a good blend of aggression and prudence.

13. Black 54: Bar/21 13/8

There's nothing spectacular or even moderately creative to be done, so Black just enters and brings down a new builder. Black doesn't play 21/16 for the same reason that White didn't play 12/18 last turn: the 16-point is a valuable, contested point, and the first person to slot it may well lose control.

Diagram 102. Black has played 54

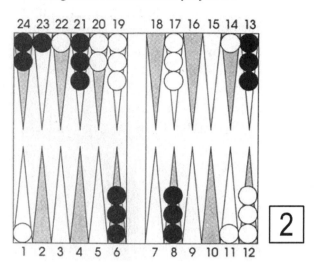

14. White 41: 14/18 17/18

White can make any of three different points with his 4-1. He chooses the 18-point. Let's see why.

One option is to make the 15-point with 11/15 10/15. This is safe and solid, cleaning up two blots, but not particularly menacing. It's a great roll for White, and he should be able to do better than this.

White can certainly make his 2-point (the 23-point) with 19/23* 22/23. Under most circumstances, this would be the natural and correct play, making an inner-board point and sending Black to the bar. But not here!

To see why, we have to understand that back games are fundamentally different from other types of backgammon games like the blitz or the race. Those games often swing wildly from roll to roll. A single turn spent dancing on the bar can mean the difference between victory and defeat. Back games, however, proceed more slowly. Once the contours of a back game have been established, the decisive part of the battle is pushed many rolls into the future. The hand-to-hand skirmishing characteristic of a blitz is postponed, while the players attempt to gain small advantages by nailing down the key points.

Suppose White does play 19/23* 22/23, and then suppose Black dances. Normally Black would be discouraged by this exchange, and White would be delighted. But here their attitude would probably be: So what? Black would still keep his two key back game points, the 21-point and the 24-point. He's almost sure to reenter sometime in the next roll or two. The crucial point in the game, when White bears his checkers in and then leaves a shot, is still many rolls in the future. In fact, a refreshing turn or two on the bar might be just what Black needs to adjust his timing.

We discussed the idea of **timing** a little bit in our first sample game (see the explanation after Diagram 45). Basically, timing is the ability to move your spare checkers for a long time (while you wait for a winning shot) without **breaking your board** (moving your checkers down to the 1, 2, and 3-points). If Black can keep his timing, he has an excellent chance to win a back game. If Black runs out of time, he's croaked.

Now let's look at the position from White's point of view. What's the best way to attack your opponent's timing? Answer - build a prime in front of his back checkers. If White can build, say, the 18 and 16-points, all those Black checkers on the 24 and 21-points may get stuck and not be able to move. White's play of making the 18-point, 14/18 17/18, looks quiet, but in reality, is far more threatening to Black than some impetuous hit.

Review the material in these last few pages carefully - all the key strategy in playing for or against a back game is explained. If you understand these ideas, you'll be way ahead of 90% of your opponents.

Diagram 103. White has played 41

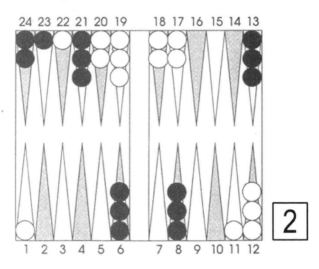

15. Black 42: 13/9 24/22*
Black keeps fighting back. He hits on the 22-point and brings a builder down to his 9-point. I think that's best, but Black had several choices with this roll, so let's look at the other options.

One play is 13/11*/7. Black hits and continues on to start his bar point. This takes away part of White's roll, but it's not very useful otherwise. Black can do better.

Black could have simply made his 4-point with 8/4 6/4. That's a solid, constructive play. The downside is that it leaves White free to pursue his own goal. He'll cover his blot on the 22-point with any three. He might also extend his prime by making the 16-point if he throws 54, 44, or 22. Rolls like 65 and 64 would cover the blot on the 22-point from the 11-point or 12-point. That's a lot of options for White.

Now let's go back to Black's actual play. Black wants to hit on the 22-point for two reasons. First, by hitting he interrupts White's plans. White has to first enter from the bar before he can make new points. Secondly, Black is trying to *upgrade his anchor*. Right now his backgame points are the 24-point and the 21-point. Black would like a different combination of points - perhaps the 21 and 22-points, or even the 21 and 23-points. Hitting on the 22 increases the chance that Black can make one of these other combinations.

What makes these other combinations of points better for a back game?

Experience has shown that back games generate the most shots later when the two points are close together. They generate the fewest shots when the points are far apart. So the worst back game is the 1-5 back game. The 1-point and the 5-point are three points apart, which is as far as you can get and still have two points in the home board.

Next worse is the 1-4 back game, where the points are separated by two other points. By trying to move his rear anchor up to the 23 or 22-point, Black is hoping to build a back game with points close together. That's good strategy.

Diagram 104. Black has played 42

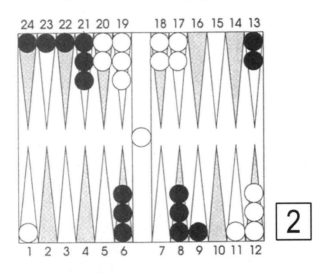

16. White 54: Bar/5/9*

White enters and hits the blot. White could create an anchor with Bar/5 1/5, which in most games would be the logical play, since the 5-point is so important. But not here. The purpose of making the defensive 5-point is to prevent your opponent from building a prime to contain your checkers. That can't happen here: most of Black's prime-building checkers are stuck on the other side of the board.

To win at backgammon, it's crucial not to fall into

stereotyped modes of thinking. The 5-point is usually very valuable, but here it's almost irrelevant.

17. Black 61: Bar/24 21/15
This one is forced, but it does allow Black to reestablish his second anchor point. With the 6, Black springs a checker into the outfield.

Diagram 105. Black has played 61

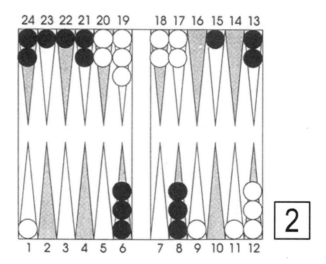

18. White 63: 9/15* 19/22*
White hits in the outfield and at the same time attacks in his inner board. He's trying to capture his 3-point (the 22-point in our diagrams), preventing Black from establishing a 3-4 back game. Good play on White's part.

19. Black 51: Bar/24
When two checkers get hit, it's often not possible to enter both at once. Here Black has to settle for getting one checker in.

20. White 43: 15/22

White could make the 15-point with this roll, but the 22-point is more important. Now the possibility of Black's making a 3-4 back game has been eliminated.

Diagram 106. White has played 43

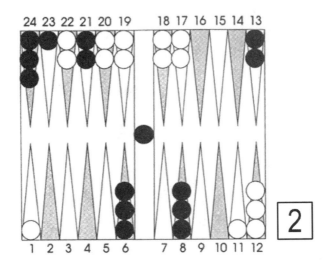

21. Black 54: Bar/21/16

Black has to enter with the 4, then look around for the best 5. He could play 13/8 or 8/3 (6/1* puts a checker out of play for no purpose), but elects to jump from behind the prime instead. This is known as **recirculation**. When you've got a bunch of checkers stuck behind a prime, it's essential to keep them moving and in play. The usual way is to move spare checkers to the most advanced of your back points (in this case, the 21-point), then launch them into the outfield at any opportunity. If they get hit, you simply try the process over again.

When playing a back game, this recirculation process is *top priority*. As a rule, it's even more important than hitting enemy blots or building points. That's just another example of how good back game strategy is completely different from what we've seen in our first two sample games. As you play, you'll discover that very few of your opponents understand these refined points. With the knowledge you're getting here, you'll be able to outplay them from either side of a back game.

Diagram 107. Black has played 54

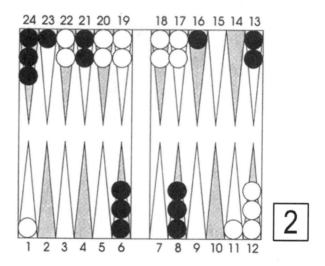

22. White 54: 11/16* 12/16

Back in the trap! White closes the fifth point of his prime, pretty much eliminating any chance Black had of winning except through a pure back game strategy. (Had White missed, it was possible that Black could have won by containing White's lone checker back on the 1-point - unlikely, but in backgammon much stranger things have happened.) Now Black is going to have to wait until White brings his men home and starts to dismantle his prime for any real winning chances to develop.

Diagram 108. White has played 54

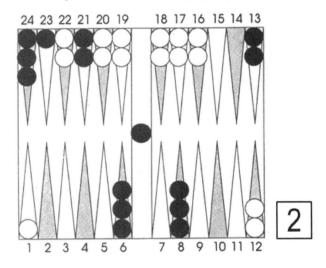

23. Black 53: Stays Out

Good news and bad news. Black would like to have rolled a 2, which would have given him three back game points, on the 24, 23, and 21-points (officially known as a 1-2-4 back game). These three-point back games are very powerful - it would be practically impossible for White to get his men home without leaving several shots along the way.

That's the bad news. The good news is that by staying out, Black doesn't have to move his men. This will probably allow him to preserve his *timing* until a shot finally emerges. Remember, it won't do Black any good to hit a shot later if his remaining men have moved all the way down to his 1, 2, and 3-points. That's called a **crushed board**, and it's nearly impossible to win from a formation like that. In fact, Black would be happy to stay on the bar for a few more turns - in that case, his timing would be secure.

Diagram 109. Black has stayed out

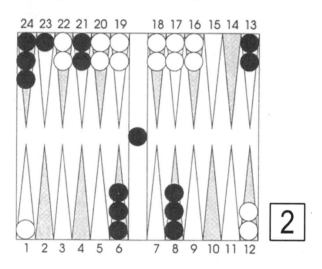

24. White 65: 12/23*
White understands the potential power of a 1-2-4 back game, so he launches a pre-emptive strike to try to eliminate that possibility.

This play is much better than the simple-minded 1/12, which brings the rear checker to safety but allows Black to throw a 2 to make the 23-point. *In backgammon, you can't afford to play by rote. You must fight for every important piece of real estate.* The most valuable point on the board right now is the 23-point. Now Black will have to throw two 2s in succession to get it.

25. Black 64: Bar/21

Again, Black can only enter one man.

Diagram 110. Black has played 64

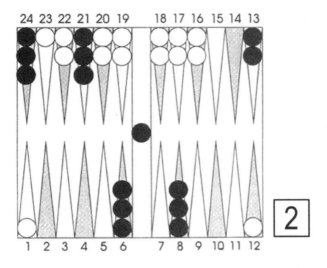

26. White 63: 12/18 1/4

With his 6, White moves into position to cover the blot on the 23-point next turn. With the 3, White prepares to escape his last man from Black's home board.

White could have covered the blot on the 23-point right away, with 17/23 17/20. However, this would have broken his prime, which right now is containing seven of Black's checkers. If Black then entered on the next turn, White's checkers on the 12-point and 1-point might have run into some trouble getting home. It's not a clear choice, and some players would have chosen to cover the 23-point right away. However, I prefer White's actual play. As long as White maintains the 5-point prime, Black will have trouble doing anything constructive.

27. Black 66: Stays out

Black's very glad he was on the bar when he rolled that number. Playing or not playing 24 pips might have made the difference between losing and preserving his timing.

Diagram 111. Black has stayed out

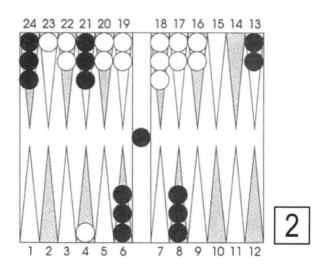

28. White 65: 4/10 18/23

At last White nails down the 23-point, committing Black to a 1-4 back game. At the same time, he brings his last checker close to home.

At this stage of a back game, there's nothing much happening. White is scooting for home, reorganizing his loose checkers and maintaining his prime as long as possible. Black will eventually enter from the bar, then build his 4, 5, and bar-points, in anticipation of a later hit. If he gets a chance, he will spring some of his *spare* checkers into White's outfield, to preserve his timing.

What's a **spare** checker? That's any checker that isn't needed to hold down a key point. Right now, Black has one spare each on the 21 and 24-points. The checker on the bar will become a second spare on one of these point as soon as it enters.

29. Black 41: Bar/21 6/5
41 is a great shot, giving Black a chance to enter on either point in White's board. Naturally, he chooses to enter on the 21-point. That way, he'll be able to free the checker with any 6 later on. With the one, he starts to build the 5-point. He could also have played 8/7, starting the bar-point. Either play of the ace is perfectly good.

30. White 63: 10/19
White brings the rear checker home to safety.

Diagram 112. White has played 63

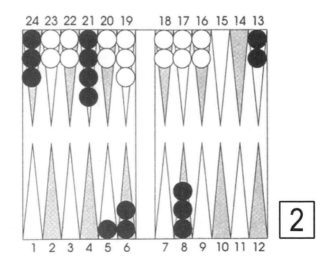

31. Black 62: 21/15 13/11

Excellent play by Black! He had a tempting alternative, 13/7/5, which would have covered the 5-point. His actual play, however, jumping out from behind the prime and creating a builder on the 11-point, is far superior. Black correctly sees that White will not leave a shot for at least one or two turns. In that time, Black will easily be able to make the 5-point. Black's real danger is the checkers stuck behind White's prime. Black needs to get those checkers mobilized and moving, which means he needs to play 21/15 with every 6 on the dice.

Once again we have an example of a key strategic idea - making the 5-point - being superceded by an idea which is more important *because of the specific conditions of the position*. This kind of flexible thinking is essential to reaching the top levels of backgammon.

Diagram 113. Black has played 62

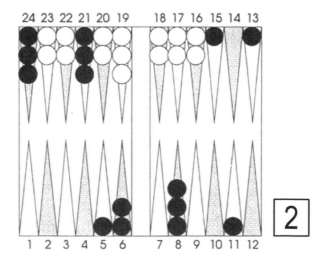

32. White 64: 16/22 16/20

White clears the back point of his prime. That's usually the right way to take down a prime - from the back. In this case, it's also the only move to avoid leaving a shot. From now on, White will try to avoid leaving a shot whenever possible. Black is in the process of controlling all the rest of the board, and a blot could be fatal.

33. Black 53: 21/16 8/5

A straightforward play. Black springs another checker for extra mobility, and covers the blot on the 5-point.

If Black's timing were dubious, he might instead play 24/21 with the three, preparing to jump the checker into the outfield. Here that's not top priority. Black's timing looks fine, and he could get a shot as early as next turn (for instance, if White rolls 64 next), so it's more important to build the 5-point.

Diagram 114. Black has played 53

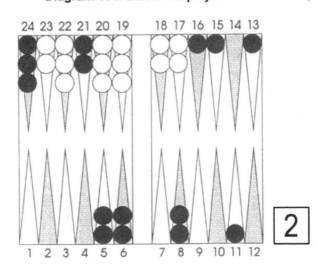

34. White 21: 18/19 18/20

Excellent technique on White's part! Based on the note to White's last move, you might expect White to play here 17/18 17/19, clearing his prime from the back. That's a good general principle, but here White sees an exception to the general rule, and artfully takes advantage of it.

The problem with 17/18 17/19 is this: White will then eventually come down to a position where he has two men on the 18-point. If White then leaves a shot while trying to clear the 18-point (with rolls like 53 or 56, for example), Black will have a *double shot* at the blot on the 18-point.

A **double shot** just means that Black will be shooting at the blot from two points within direct range - in this case, the 21 and 24-points. Black will be able to hit with any 6 or any 3 on the dice. He'll actually be a favorite to hit the blot.

Now look what happens if White clears the 18-point instead, leaving the 17-point behind. If White later leaves a shot while trying to clear the 17-point, it will only be a *single shot*; Black will only be able to hit it directly from the 21-point. Black will be much less likely to hit.

By looking a roll or two ahead, White has shrewdly reduced his overall risk. *Intelligent risk management* is one of the keys to winning backgammon.

Diagram 115. White has played 21

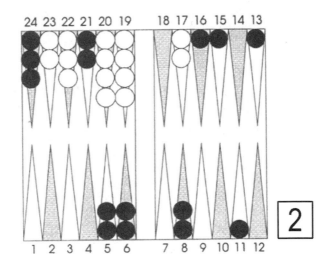

35. Black 65: 13/7 15/10

Having made the 5-point, Black now has to decide in what order to make further points. He correctly decides to go after the 7-point next. He could try to make the 4-point by playing 15/4. However, the 4-point is harder to make than the 7-point, and it's also not directly part of a 4-point prime.

Black wants to build a prime of either four, five, or six consecutive points, so that when he hits a shot, the checker will be trapped. The easiest and quickest prime for Black to build is the one that includes the points he already has (the 5, 6, and 8) and which stretches back into the outfield (since Black's builders are closest to the outfield). That means Black's next two target points are the 7-point and the 9-point.

36. White 65: 17/23 17/22
Nice shot. White has successfully cleared his outfield points, and he's ready to start bearing off.

37. Black 31: 10/7 16/15
Black makes the 7-point, completing a 4-point prime, while the checker on the 15-point now bears directly on the next target point, the 9-point.

38. White 65: 19/off 20/off
A forced play, bearing off two checkers.

Diagram 116. White has played 65

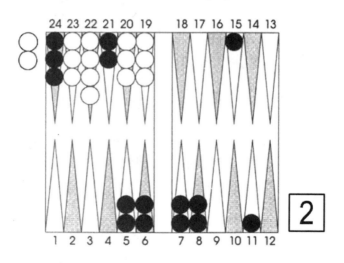

39. Black 52: 15/10 11/9
Black continues with the strategic idea. By slotting the 9-point, he is prepared to make a 5-point prime next turn if he rolls an ace.

40. White 61: 19/off 22/23

The only way to play the number without leaving a shot. Bearoffs against contact (your opponent still holds one or two points in your home board) typically offer little scope for creativity: almost all the plays will be forced. The idea is just to avoid leaving a shot for as long as possible.

Diagram 117. White has played 61

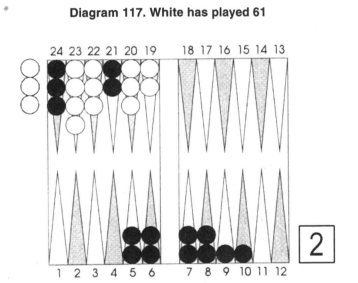

41. Black 62: 24/18/16

Black can't make any progress building his prime, so he springs his last spare checker. His timing for the backgame is ideal - he'll almost certainly be able to build a solid prime if he hits a checker. Unfortunately, if he doesn't hit a shot, he'll certainly be gammoned or backgammoned.

42. White 52: 20/off 23/off

No other legal play.

43. Black 32: 16/11

Black wanted to throw a one or a seven, to make the 9-point and complete five points in a row. No such luck. Instead, Black leaves the 9-point slotted (hoping to cover next turn with ones or twos).

44. White 62: 19/off 23/off

White has skirted problems for several turns now, but lightning finally strikes as White leaves a double shot. (It could have been much worse - 65 would have left a quadruple shot at two blots!)

Diagram 118. White has played 62

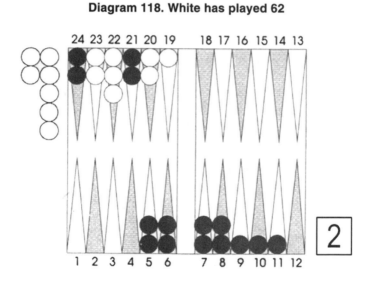

Black is now actually a favorite to hit. Of his 36 possible throws, fully 20 (all throws containing a 5 or a 2) hit the blot on the 19-point.

Should Black redouble? Not at all! Let's see why.

Many beginners confuse *hitting shots* with *winning games*. Suppose you knew that Black was going to hit this shot. Would that guarantee that Black was going to win? Absolutely not. Don't forget, White has already taken off seven checkers. That's a lot of checkers.

Black could hit this checker, complete a full 6-point prime, roll the prime home and close out his board, start bearing off checkers, and still lose! All White has to do is enter when Black starts to open up points in his board, and he could easily scoot around the board and win.

In order to win this game, Black has to do four things, one after the other:

First, he has to hit this shot.

Second, he has to complete a 6-point prime, so that White's checker can't escape the trap.

Third, he has to roll the prime home and close out his home board, putting White's trapped checker on the bar.

Finally, Black has to bear off quickly, so that he can win the race even after White eventually enters his man.

Here's a key concept that all top backgammon players understand: *The likelihood of doing two things, one after the other, is the probability of doing the first thing multiplied by the probability of doing the second thing.*

For example, if the probability of doing A (say, hitting a blot) is 90%, and the probability of doing B (say, winning after hitting) is 90%, the probability of doing A and B, one after the other, is only 90% times 90%, or 81%.

Be sure you understand this concept. If you do, you'll be way ahead of most of your opponents, and you'll be well on your way to being a shrewd doubler and an even shrewder taker.

What this means, basically, is that if you have to do several things to win the game, and you're a favorite to do each one, you may still be a solid underdog to do all of them together.

Let's go back to our position in the game. We listed four things that Black had to do to win. Let's make a rough guess at how likely he is to do each one, then multiply those numbers together to see how likely he is to win. (Pay attention - you may be very surprised at the result!)

First, Black has to hit this shot. The chances of that, as we explained earlier, is 20 out of 36 - that's about 55%.

Second, Black has to complete a 6-point prime, trapping White's checker. He's got four points already, with slotted checkers on the fifth and sixth points. After Black hits, however, White will have numbers like 36, 45, and 46 to enter and pop out. And that's just the first turn! I'm going to guess that Black's chances are about 70% to make a prime and trap White.

Third, Black has to roll his prime home, filling in the 4, 3, 2, and 1-points in order while keeping six points in a row. That's actually easier than it might look. With good technique, I'll give Black a 95% chance to succeed here.

Fourth, Black has to win after closing his board, given that White already has seven checkers off. Experience tells us that Black is a favorite to do this, but not by much. Perhaps he's 60% in this case.

Black is a favorite to do each and every thing on this list, but what are his chances of doing all four things, one after another? Get out your calculators and multiple 0.55 by 0.70 by 0.95 by 0.60. You should get 0.22. That 22%, or less than one chance in four! Not too good, and certainly no reason to be doubling.

Study this example carefully. A lot of doubling and taking decisions will depend on reasoning just like you saw here. If you understand this method, you'll be way ahead of 90% of the people you play and on your way to playing winning backgammon.

45. Black 21: 21/19* 10/9
A great shot for Black, hitting while making the fifth point in his prime.

46. White 32: Bar/3 20/22
And a poor shot for White! The rules require you to play your whole number, so White has to enter and expose another blot in his board. (He could also play Bar/2 20/23, which wouldn't really make any difference.) Black's well-timed back game is showing its power.

Diagram 119. White has played 32

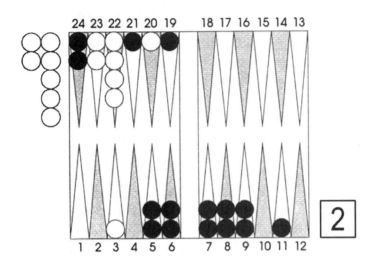

47. Black doubles to 4.

Pressure doubling! At the very moment when White feels his game is suddenly in jeopardy, Black ships over the cube. Excellent.

Doubling the previous turn, as we saw, involved no pressure at all. The position was an easy take and almost any player in White's position would have snapped up the cube. Now, however it's a different story. Black is a clear favorite and can become a huge favorite if he hits the second checker. A great double on Black's part.

48. White takes.

Not to be intimidated, White shows his rock-solid determination by taking. Despite the danger, White figures he has two ways to win:

• Black could miss the shot at the second checker, and White could eventually win based on the seven checkers he has already borne off.

• Black could hit the second checker, but White could form an anchor on the 2, 3, or 4-points. This anchor could give Black some problems as he tries to bear in.

Remember that to take a double, White only needs to win one game in four. That's often easier to do than you might think, even in positions that look unpromising. As you progress in backgammon, you'll get better and better at assessing these chances. For now, keep one simple rule in mind - *when in doubt, take*.

49. Black 63: 19/10
Black misses the blot on the 20-point. His attention now must focus on containing White's single checker. He uses the 63 to slot the 10-point, the last point he needs to complete a 6-point prime. Next turn, if he rolls an ace or a 65, he can cover this point.

Perhaps you're asking "But suppose White rolls a 61? Won't that hit the blot?" The answer is yes, but that's a risk Black *must* take. In backgammon, you can't be a winner by worrying about the 17-1 or 35-1 long shots.

You have to build a position and play against your opponent's *most likely* rolls. Only after you've built up an overwhelming advantage should you worry about preventing the long shots. Right now, Black has some work to do just to make sure he's a favorite in the game. That means building a six-point prime is top priority.

50. White 31: 3/4 20/23

A good shot. White picks up the blot on the 20-point, leaving only one checker to worry about, and moves his straggler up to the 21-point, ready to leap the prime.

Diagram 120. White has played 31

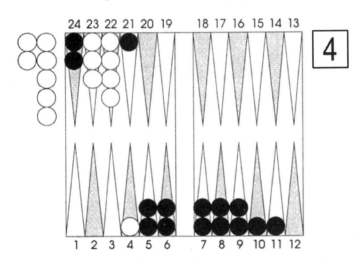

51. Black 64: 10/4* 11/7

Black wanted to complete his prime, but didn't throw the ace that would let him do so. Hitting with the six is now mandatory. Black can't let White sit unmolested on the 4-point, ready to run into the outfield. This way, White needs a four, followed by a six, to get away.

Playing 11/7 gives Black a direct cover for the blot on the 4-point. If White doesn't roll a 4, and Black then rolls a 3, Black will play 7/4 and complete his prime.

52. White 62: Bar/2

Forced play.

Diagram 121. White has played 62

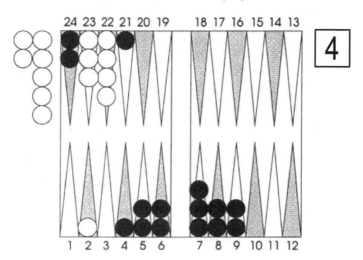

53. Black 63: 7/4 24/18

Success! Black completes his prime, putting him back in control. As long as he doesn't break his formation of six points in a row, White's lone straggler can never escape.

By playing 24/18 rather than 21/15, Black sets another little tactical trap. If White rolls 32, 42, 52, or 62 next turn, he will be forced to play 22/24*, exposing a second checker which Black might hit. Be alert for these small tactical plays, especially in the endgame.

When you have control of the game, try to visualize how your opponent's different numbers will play, and move to take maximum advantage.

54. White 54: No move

White is only in position to play ones and twos on the dice. With larger numbers, he has to forfeit his turn.

Diagram 122. White could not play

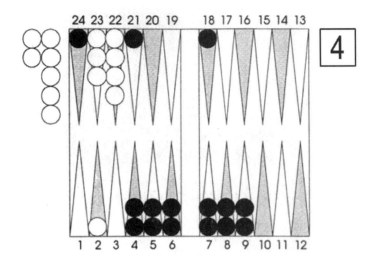

55. Black 33: 9/3(2)
A nice roll which lets Black *roll his prime* forward one space. Black still maintains a full prime, but now it's closer to home.

56. White 65: No move
As before, White can't play.

Diagram 123. White could not play

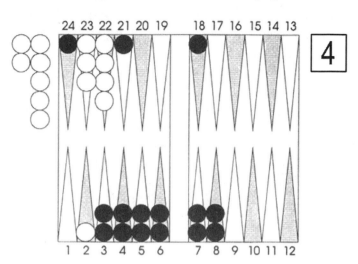

57. Black 65: 18/7
Fine play. Black brings a new attacker into play.

Black had a chance to make a terrible blunder. He could have played the superficial 8/2* 7/2, marching his prime forward one more pip, at the cost of giving White a 61 from the bar to leap out and hit on the 7-point.

Don't fall into this trap! I once saw a whole tournament lost on just this mistake. Keep your 6-point prime, bring up the reserves, and use your spare checkers to move the prime forward. Remember: as long as you keep six points in a row, White can't escape.

58. White 44: No move

59. Black 55: 7/2* 21/6

Black hits at the front of his prime, and brings a spare into covering range. If White doesn't throw a two, Black can cover and keep his prime by throwing a six or a four. Excellent technique.

60. White 43: Stays out

Diagram 124. White stayed out

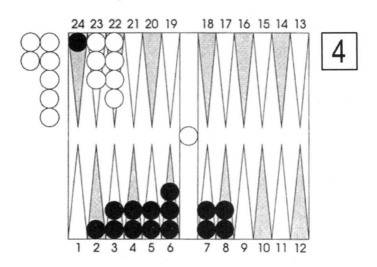

61. Black 63: 8/2 8/5

Black naturally covers, rolling his prime forward one more pip. Playing the three from the 8-point to the 5-point shows Black's excellent technique in operation again. Black stays back on the 24-point in case White's next throw is 21. In that case, White will enter with the one and hit on the 24-point with the two, exposing another blot. Black is relentlessly alert to anything that might give him an extra edge.

62. White 32: Stays out

Diagram 125. White stayed out

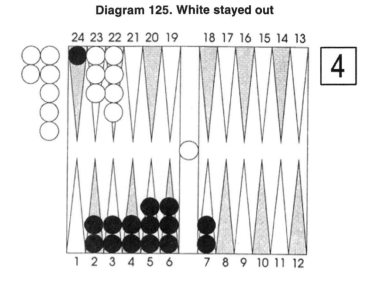

63. Black 53: 24/21 6/1

Black prepares to move the prime forward one last time by *slotting the front of the prime*. If White fails to hit, Black can complete the closeout by rolling any six or any four. If White does hit, he still can't escape from Black's 6-point prime. Black will just reenter his checker, move it around the board, and try again.

64. White 62: Stays out

65. Black 52: 21/14

Black can't cover his blot, so he brings up the reinforcements.

66. White 54: Stays out

Diagram 126. White stayed out

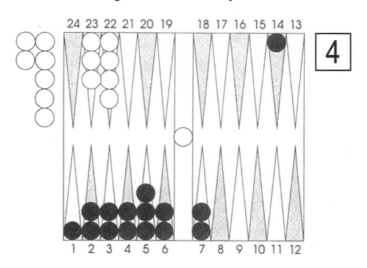

67. Black 63: 7/1 14/11

Mission accomplished! Black has succeeded in rolling his prime all the way home, making a closed board. Now White can't even roll until Black opens up a point in the board.

What is Black's strategy for the next few rolls? Basically, it's pretty simple. He should bring his spare checkers (currently on the 7 and 11-points) in to his home board. He should try to arrange them on the high points in his board - the 4, 5, and 6 points would be ideal. Then he wants to bear off as many of his spares as possible before opening a point in his board.

Remember, White already has seven checkers borne off. Even though White still has to enter his checker and move it all the way around the board, that seven-checker lead is important.

68. Black 31: 11/8 7/6
According to plan. Black puts a spare on the 6-point, and brings the last checker closer to home.

69. Black 42: 8/4/2
Actually, Black would rather not play the two. His formation of spares on the three highest points in his board is ideal. But he has no choice. The next couple of throws will be very important.

Diagram 127. Black has played 42

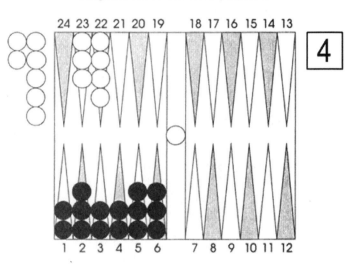

70. Black 61: 6/off 5/4
Now we see the importance of putting a spare on the 6-point. If Black didn't have a spare there, this roll (or any other roll containing a 6) would have forced him to open the 6-point, finally giving White a chance to enter. In situations like this, it's crucial for Black to keep his board closed as long as possible.

71. Black 63: 6/off 6/3

Black rolls another six and bears off a checker, but has to open the 6-point in his board. Naturally, he safeties the blot on the 6-point with 6/3. If White stays out this first turn (and he's a big favorite to do so), Black will become a commanding favorite in the game. If White enters, it's anybody's game.

72. White 63: Bar/6/9

White enters quickly, and now the complexion of the game has changed dramatically. If Black doesn't roll a double, White will have to think about turning the cube!

73. Black 31: 3/off 1/off

A feeble shot on Black's part. White's getting a gleam in his eye ...

Diagram 128. Black has played 31

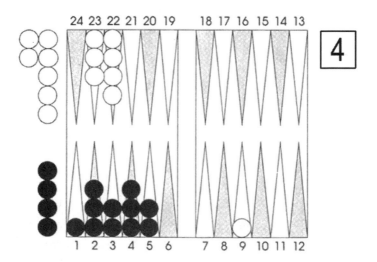

74. White doubles to 8

White doesn't hesitate but sends the cube back to the 8-level. White knows he's a favorite, and doesn't mind playing for higher stakes.

Should White have doubled? Should Black take? Let's take a look at how we might figure this out.

We're now in a kind of game called a **straight race**. There are no more fancy strategies of blocking or containment left. Both sides have broken contact with each other, and are racing to the finish line. Whoever throws the biggest numbers now will win, except that the side closer to the finish line has the advantage.

The best way to evaluate a race is to do what's called a **pip count**. In a pip count, we figure out how many pips each side must throw on the dice to bear off all remaining checkers exactly. (Throwing a 4 and a 3 on the dice totals 7 pips, for instance.) By comparing the pip counts for the two sides, we can not only find out who's ahead, but often whether the position is a double or a take.

We'll start by computing the pip count for White, who is on roll. White has one man in the outfield on the 9-point. That man has to travel 10 pips to get to the 19-point (White's 6-point), and then 6 more pips to get off, so he's 16 pips away from bearing off. White has four men on the 22-point (White's own 3-point), each of whom needs 3 pips to bear off. And finally White has three men on the 23-point, representing 2 pips each.

White's total pip count is 16 pips for the man in the outfield, 12 pips for the four men on his 3-point, and 6 pips for the three men on his 2-point, or 34 pips overall.

We calculate Black's pip count in a similar manner. Two men on the 5-point are 10 pips; three men on the 4-point are 12 pips; two men on the 3-point are 6 pips; three men on the 2-point are another 6 pips; and one man on the 1-point is a final pip. The total is $10 + 12 + 6 + 6 + 1$, or 35 pips.

So White needs to throw 34 pips on the dice to bear off his 8 checkers, while Black needs 35 pips to bear off his 11 checkers. What are we to make of this?

The basic rule of thumb that governs doubling in most racing situations is this:

In longer races, the leader needs to lead by about 8% in the pip count to double. The trailer needs to be within 12% to take.

As the race gets shorter, down around about 25 pips for both sides, the leader can double as long as he's even in the race. (The reason it's OK to double with an even pip count is because being able to roll first is a significant advantage all by itself.)

What does that say about our race? The race is pretty short, but it's still not in the 25-pip range. A 10% lead in a 35-pip race would be 3.5 pips; an 8% lead might be more like 3 pips. White leads by only 1 pip. He's a favorite, but it's starting to look like his double might be a little too soon. At any rate, probably an easy take for Black. Still, the cube is going to the 8-level, and many players might get scared of losing 8 points and drop:

75. Black takes.

Not Black. He understands another basic principle of doubling: *If a cube would be a take going from 1 to 2, then it's a take going from 4 to 8 (or any higher level.)*

76. White 52: 9/16

A larger number would have been better, but White will settle for this. Next turn he's ready to run home and start bearing off.

77. Black 21: 2/off 1/off

Black rolls his worst: only three pips, and now he has a gap on the 1-point. One nice thing about taking a cube, though, is that you get to play the game through to the end, no matter how bad your position gets. There's always a chance to save the game with a spectacular double if all strategy fails.

Diagram 129. Black has played 21

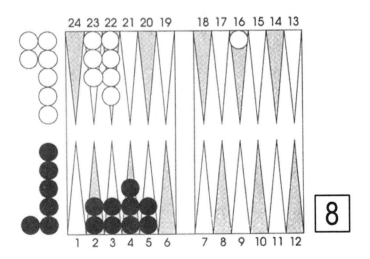

78. White 51: 16/21 23/24

White, in turn, throws an awkward number. He's able to reach his home board with the 5, but with no checkers on the 24-point, he can't bear anyone off with the 1.

White's play of the ace from the 23-point to the 24-point is excellent and illustrates an important principle of bear-off play: ***Bear off a checker whenever you can; if you can't, fill in a gap.***

White's open 24-point is what's called a **gap**: a point with no checkers on it. When you roll a number corresponding to a gap, you're going to miss bearing off a checker, so it's good to fill gaps whenever possible.

79. Black 44: 4/off(3) 5/1

Great shot! Black is able to bear off three checkers from the 4-point, then has to move a checker down to the 1-point for his last four. He moves a lot of checkers, but most important, he leaves himself with only six checkers and a realistic chance to be off in three more turns.

80. White 65: 21/off 22/off

A pretty good throw for White, who gets down to six checkers himself.

Diagram 130. White has played 65

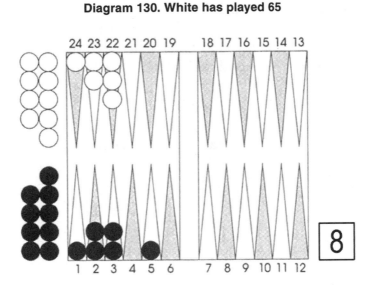

Should Black now double? No. He has the same number of checkers as White, but he trails in the pip count, 16 to 14. As we said before, you generally want to be even in the pip count to double in these very short pip count situations. So Black is correct to wait.

81. Black 31: 3/off 1/off
A poor shot, and now Black is very glad he held onto the cube last turn.

82. White 65: 22/off(2)
White is throwing big numbers, but with his checkers on the low points they don't do anything special. White is a solid favorite in the game, as most of Black's aces and fours next turn fail to take a checker off.

83. Black 53: 5/off 3/off

A great shot for Black, taking off two checkers. Unless White can bear off all four checkers (by throwing 33, 44, 55, or 66), Black will be thinking of doubling next turn!

84. White 31: 22/off 24/off

Diagram 131. White has played 31

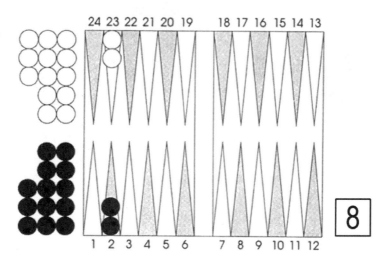

85. Black Doubles to 16

The advantage is now firmly with Black, and he cranks up the tension another notch, turning the cube to 16 on White's side of the table!

An excellent double on Black's part. With only two checkers left on each side, we can start to estimate each side's chances just by looking at the possible rolls next turn. Of Black's 36 different dice rolls, all but 10 win immediately for him. (The 10 are the rolls that contain an ace: 61 and 16, 51 and 15, 41 and 14, 31 and 13, 21 and 12.) That gives him 26 winning rolls and 10 that don't win, making him 72% to win. That's enough to give him a solid double.

White, on the other hand, still has a take! Black is only 72% to bear both checkers off, which means White is still in the game 28% of the time. That's more than the 25% he needs to take, so he can take and play on. And as we explained before, the level of the cube doesn't matter. A take is still a take.

86. Black 41: 2/off 2/1

A heartbreaking roll for Black, but that's not the worst of it.

Diagram 132. Black has played 41

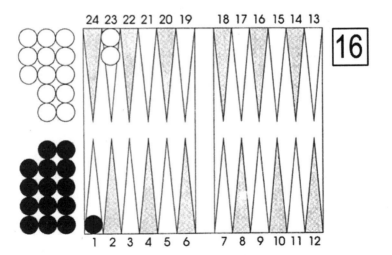

87. White doubles to 32.

White sends the cube up another notch, to 32! We don't need to worry about the correctness of this double - White's reasoning is exactly the same as Black's a turn ago. He wins with 26 numbers, loses with 10. He must double, and Black must take. One way or another, this extraordinary game is about to draw to a close.

88. Black takes.

This is it.

89. White rolls 61 and loses 32 points.

A heartbreaker for White, a thriller for Black. This game gives you some idea of the amazing swings that are possible in backgammon. That's part of what makes it the incredibly great game that it is. Despite the swings, the edge always goes to the player who can blend knowledge and nerve to outwit and outlast his opponent.

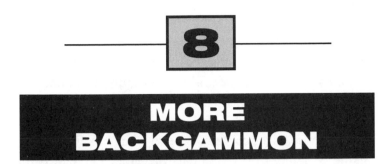

MORE BACKGAMMON

CHOUETTES

The simplest way to play backgammon is to sit down against a single opponent and play for an afternoon or evening. If you join a backgammon club, however, you may often find that several people all want to play at once. Rather than break into several separate games (which would leave someone out if the number of players was odd), players will organize what is called a *chouette*. A **chouette** is just a way for several people to participate in one game of backgammon. It is a more social way of playing, very popular at backgammon clubs around the country.

To start a chouette, all the players roll for high dice. The player with the highest dice is the **box**. The player with the second highest dice is the **captain**. All other players are part of the **team**, and they assist the captain. The box now plays a game against the captain, with the members of the team joining the captain in the play. The captain, however, rolls the dice and has the final say on all plays. The captain and all players on the team have separate cubes, all of which begin the game at the 1-level.

All players control their own doubling cube. When it is the box's turn, he may elect to double the captain and all the team members, or just certain players, or no one. If several players are doubled, they each make separate decisions on whether to take or drop. When the captain is *on roll*, players can decide individually to double the box or not.

If the box beats the captain, he retains the box for the next game, whether or not he beats the other players. If the captain wins, he becomes the box for the next game and the former box player moves down to the bottom of the line. All other players move up, with the second player on the team becoming the new captain. Players can leave or join a chouette at any time. A new player starts at the bottom of the rotation.

CLUBS AND TOURNAMENTS
The best way to meet other backgammon enthusiasts is at a backgammon club or a backgammon tournament. There are many clubs around the country, usually at least one in every major city. Clubs meet once or twice a week in a hotel or a restaurant and usually run small tournaments where beginners can get started.

There are also many backgammon tournaments at the local, regional, national, and even international level. Regional tournaments in the United States usually attract between 100 and 200 players, and are held over a long weekend. International tournaments are gala affairs, with hundreds of participants from around the world, black-tie dinners, main and side events, and prize funds which can reach hundreds of thousands of dollars.

The two most prestigious events in the world are the

World Championship, held every July in Monte Carlo, and the World Cup, held every other year in an American city. The winners of these tournaments are usually among the world's very best players.

For a complete and current list of clubs around the United States, write to:

<u>The Gammon Press</u>, P.O. Box 294, Arlington, MA 02174. Include $1 for postage and handling.

MAKING FURTHER PROGRESS

That brings us just about to the end of this book. If you're like most people, you probably want to go out and try your hand at this game. That's good: go to it. If you can't find enough players in your town, teach some of your friends to play. They might be reluctant at first. Don't worry, that's natural. Most folks are a little leery about trying new things. Keep after them, and chances are that pretty soon you'll have a group of players just as avid as you are.

What's next? If you like reading, there's a lot of books about backgammon and its finer points. I have written two other backgammon books for Cardoza Publishing, *Backgammon for Serious Players* and *501 Essential Backgammon Problems*, both of which you'll find helpful in making you a much better player.

If there are organized clubs and tournaments in your area, pay them a visit. You won't have to play at first– most clubs welcome newcomers, and they won't mind if you just sit and watch. Ask the director who the best players are, then go and observe their game. Try to pick up some pointers by watching what they do. If you have questions, it's not such a good idea to ask the players themselves. Some people get quite intense while they're playing, and don't always welcome questions from the spectators. Ask a director, or, if there's a crowd watching, one of the other spectators. After that, it's up to you.

Good luck!

GLOSSARY

Automatic Double - An optional rule to increase the stakes in game. If both players roll the same number on the dice to start the game, they may agree to turn the doubling cube to "2" for that game before rolling over.

Backgammon - A triple game, which occurs when one player bears off all his checkers while his opponent still has at least one checker on the bar or in the first player's home board. Also, the name of the game.

Bar - The raised vertical strip running down the center of a backgammon board. Checkers which are hit are placed on the bar, and must reenter the game in the opponent's inner board before any other checkers can be moved.

Bear Off - Removing checkers from the board. A player can only bear off after all 15 of his checkers have been moved to his inner board.

Blitz - A game plan which involves attacking the opponent's checkers and trying to build a closed home board at the same time.

Blot - A single checker on a point, which is vulnerable to being hit by the opponent.

Checkers - The playing pieces. Each side has 15 checkers to start the game.

Closed Board - A situation where one player has made the six points in his home board. If he then hits one of his opponent's checkers, that checker will not be able to reenter the game until the first player opens up ("breaks") his home board.

Doubles - Rolling the same number on both dice. Doubles allow the player to move that number four times.

Doubling Cube - The large die numbered "2" through "64" in powers of 2. The doubling cube controls the number of points at risk in the game.

Gammon - A double game, which occurs when one player bears off all his checkers while his opponent fails to bear off any checkers.

Hit - Moving to a point where the opponent has only one checker ("blot"). The hit checker is placed on the bar.

Home Board - The six points for each player which are the jumping-off locations for the bearoff. In our diagrams, Black's home board are the points labelled 1-6; White's home board are the points 19-24.

Points - The triangular markers on a backgammon board; also, two or more checkers together on the same point, which constitute a "made point".

Prime - A series of consecutive blocking points. A "full prime" is six points in a row.

GLOSSARY

Quadrant - One of the four quarters of the backgammon board.

Single Game - The simplest and most common form of victory, which occurs when a player bears off all his checkers while his opponent has borne off some, but not all, of his checkers.

Slot - To deliberately place a blot on a point, hoping to make that point on a future roll.

CARDOZA PUBLISHING ONLINE
www.cardozapub.com

We welcome your suggestions and comments, and are glad to have you as a customer. Our philosophy is to bring you the best quality chess and backgammon books from the top authors and authorities in the chess world, featuring *words* (as opposed to hieroglyphics), *clear explanations* (as opposed to gibberish), *nice presentations* (as opposed to books simply slapped together), and authoritative information. And all this at reasonable prices.

We hope you like the results.

Don't forget to try out the many other books in the Cardoza Publishing library. To find out about our newest books or to order backgammon and chess sets, chess clocks or other accessories:

- Go online: www.cardozapub.com
- Use email: cardozapub@aol.com
- Call toll free: (800)577-9467

FREE - CHESS CITY MAGAZINE
www.chesscity.com

Go online now to visit our free online chess magazine with articles, columns, gossip, and more. The web's most interesting and informative chess magazine is free to you from Cardoza Publishing!
